THE CORNER HOUSE GIRLS AT SCHOOL

GRACE BROOKS HILL

1st WORLD
LIBRARY
Literary Society

The Corner House Girls at School

Grace Brooks Hill

© 1st World Library, 2007
PO Box 2211
Fairfield, IA 52556
www.1stworldlibrary.com
First Edition

LCCN: 2007930788

Softcover ISBN: 978-1-4218-4830-3
Hardcover ISBN: 978-1-4218-4733-7
eBook ISBN: 978-1-4218-4927-0

Purchase *"The Corner House Girls at School"*
as a traditional bound book at:
www.1stWorldLibrary.com/purchase.asp?ISBN=978-1-4218-4830-3

1st World Library is a literary, educational organization
dedicated to:

- Creating a free internet library of downloadable ebooks

- Hosting writing competitions and offering book publishing
  scholarships.

1ˢᵗ World Library Literary Society

Giving Back to the World

"If you want to work on the core problem, it's early school literacy."

- James Barksdale, former CEO of Netscape

"No skill is more crucial to the future of a child, or to a democratic and prosperous society, than literacy."

- Los Angeles Times

"Literacy... means far more than learning how to read and write... The aim is to transmit... knowledge and promote social participation."

- UNESCO

"Literacy is not a luxury, it is a right and a responsibility. If our world is to meet the challenges of the twenty-first century we must harness the energy and creativity of all our citizens."

- President Bill Clinton

"Parents should be encouraged to read to their children, and teachers should be equipped with all available techniques for teaching literacy, so the varying needs and capacities of individual kids can be taken into account."

- Hugh Mackay

CONTENTS

CHAPTER I

A GOAT, FOUR GIRLS, AND A PIG

When Sam Pinkney brought Billy Bumps over to the old
Corner House, and tied him by the corner of the woodshed,
there was at once a family conclave called. Sam was never
known to be into anything but mischief; therefore when he
gravely presented the wise looking old goat to Tess,
suspicion was instantly aroused in the Kenway household
that there was something beside good will behind Master
Sam's gift.

"Beware of the Greeks when they come bearing gifts,"
Agnes freely translated.

"But you know very well, Aggie, Sammy Pinkney is not a
Greek. He's Yankee—like us. That's a Greek man that sells
flowers down on Main Street," said Tess, with gravity.

"What I said is allegorical," pronounced Agnes, loftily.

"We know Allie Neuman—Tess and me," ventured Dot, the
youngest of the Corner House girls. "She lives on Willow
Street beyond Mrs. Adams' house, and she is going to be in
my grade at school."

"Oh, fine, Ruth!" cried Agnes, the twelve-year-old, suddenly seizing the eldest sister and dancing her about the big dining-room. "Won't it be just *fine* to get to school again?"

"Fine for me," admitted Ruth, who had missed nearly two years of school attendance, and was now going to begin again in her proper grade at the Milton High School.

"Eva Larry says we'll have the very nicest teacher there is— Miss Shipman. This is Eva's last year in grammar school, too, you know. We'll graduate together," said Agnes.

Interested as Tess and Dot were in the prospect of attending school in Milton for the first time, just now they had run in to announce the arrival of Mr. Billy Bumps.

"And a very suggestive name, I must say," said Ruth, reflectively. "I don't know about that Pinkney boy. Do you suppose he is playing a joke on you, Tess?"

"Why, no!" cried the smaller girl. "How could he? *For the goat's there.*"

"Maybe that's the joke," suggested Agnes.

"Well, we'll go and see him," said Ruth. "But there must be some reason beside good-will that prompted that boy to give you such a present."

"I know," Dot said, solemnly.

"What is it, Chicken-little?" demanded the oldest sister, pinching the little girl's cheek.

"Their new minister," proclaimed Dot.

"Their *what*?" gasped Agnes.

"Who, dear?" asked Ruth.

"Mrs. Pinkney's new minister. She goes to the Kaplan Chapel," said Dot, gravely, "and they got a new minister there. He came to call at Mrs. Pinkney's and the goat wasn't acquainted with him."

"Oh-ho!" giggled Agnes. "Light on a dark subject."

"Who told you, child?" asked Tess, rather doubtfully.

"Holly Pease. And she said that Billy Bumps butted the new minister right through the cellar window—the coal window."

"My goodness!" ejaculated Ruth. "Did it hurt him?"

"They'd just put in their winter's coal, and he went head first into that," said Dot. "So he didn't fall far. But he didn't dare go out of the house again until Sam came home after school and shut Billy up. Holly says Billy Bumps camped right outside the front door and kept the minister a prisoner."

The older girls were convulsed with laughter at this tale, but Ruth repeated: "We might as well go and see him. If he is *very* savage—"

"Oh, he isn't!" cried Tess and Dot together. "He's just as tame!"

The four sisters started for the yard, but in the big kitchen Mrs. MacCall stopped them. Mrs. MacCall was housekeeper and she mothered the orphaned Kenway girls and seemed much nearer to them than Aunt Sarah Maltby, who sat most of her time in the big front room upstairs, seldom speaking to her nieces.

Mrs. MacCall was buxom, gray-haired—and every hair was martialed just *so*, and all imprisoned in a cap when the good lady was cooking. She was looking out of one of the rear windows when the girls trooped through.

"For the land sakes!" ejaculated Mrs. MacCall. "What's that goat doing in our yard?"

"It's our goat," explained Tess.

"What?"

"Yes, ma'am," said Dot, seriously. "He's a very nice goat. He has a real noble beard—don't you think?"

"A goat!" repeated Mrs. MacCall. "What next? A goat is the very last thing I could ever find a use for in this world. But I s'pose the Creator knew what He was about when He made them."

"I think they're lots of fun," said roly-poly Agnes, giggling again.

"Fun! Ah! what's that he's eatin' this very minute?" screamed Mrs. MacCall, and she started for the door.

She led the way to the porch, and immediately plunged down the steps into the yard. "My stocking!" she shrieked. "The very best pair I own. Oh, dear! Didn't I say a goat was a perfectly useless thing?"

It was a fact that a limp bit of black rag hung out of the side of Billy Bumps' mouth. A row of stockings hung on a line stretched from the corner of the woodshed and the goat had managed to reach the first in the row.

"Give it up, you beast!" exclaimed Mrs. MacCall, and grabbed the toe of the stocking just as it was about to disappear.

She yanked and Billy disgorged the hose. He had chewed it to pulp, evidently liking the taste of the dye. Mrs. MacCall threw the thing from her savagely and Billy lowered his head, stamped his feet, and threatened her with his horns.

"Oh, I'm so sorry, Mrs. MacCall!" cried Ruth, soothingly.

"That won't bring back my stocking," declared the house-keeper. "Half a pair of stockings—humph! that's no good to anybody, unless it's a person with a wooden leg."

"I'll get you a new pair, Mrs. MacCall," said Tess. "Of course, I'm sort of responsible for Billy, for he was given to me."

"You'll be bankrupt, I'm afraid, Tess," chuckled Agnes, "if you try to make good for all the damage a goat can do."

"But it won't cost much to keep him," said Tess, eagerly. "You know, they live on tin cans, and scraps, and thistles, and all sorts of *cheap* things."

"Those stockings weren't cheap," declared the housekeeper as she took her departure. "They cost seventy-five cents."

"Half your month's allowance, Tess," Dot reminded her, with awe. "Oh, dear, me! Maybe Billy Bumps will be expensive, after all."

"Say! Ruth hasn't said you can keep him yet," said Agnes.

"He looks dangerous to me. He has a bad eye."

"Why! he's just as kind!" cried Tess, and immediately walked up to the old goat. At once Billy stopped shaking his head, looked up, and bleated softly. He was evidently assured of the quality of Tess Kenway's kindness.

"He likes me," declared Tess, with conviction.

"Glo-ree!" ejaculated a deep and unctuous voice, on the heels of Tess' declaration. "Wha's all dis erbout—heh! Glo-ree! Who done let dat goat intuh disher yard? Ain' dat Sam Pinkney's ol' Billy?"

A white-haired, broadly smiling old negro, stooped and a bit lame with rheumatism, but otherwise spry, came from the rear premises of the old Corner House, and stopped to roll his eyes, first glancing at the children and then at the goat.

"Whuffor all disher combobberation? Missee Ruth! Sho' ain' gwine tuh take dat ole goat tuh boa'd, is yo'?"

"I don't know what to do, Uncle Rufus," declared Ruth Kenway, laughing, yet somewhat disturbed in her mind. She was a dark, straight-haired girl, with fine eyes and a very intelligent face. She was not pretty like Agnes; yet she was a very attractive girl.

"Oh! we want to keep him!" wailed Dot. She, too, boldly approached Billy Bumps. It seemed as though the goat knew both the smaller Kenway girls, for he did not offer to draw away from them.

"I 'spect Mr. Pinkney made dat Sam git rid ob de ole goat," grumbled Uncle Rufus, who was a very trustworthy servant and had lived for years at the old Corner House before the four Kenway sisters came to dwell there. "I reckon he's a bad goat," added the old man.

"He doesn't look very wicked just now," suggested Agnes.

"But where can we keep a goat?" demanded Ruth.

"Dot used to think one lived in the garret," said Tess, smiling. "But it was only a ghost folks thought lived there— and we know there aren't any such things as ghosts *now*."

"Don' yo' go tuh 'spressin' ob you' 'pinion too frequent erbout sperits, chile," warned Uncle Rufus, rolling his eyes again. "Dere may hab been no ghos' in de garret; but dere's ghos'es somewhars—ya-as'm. Sho' is!"

"I don't really see how we can keep him," said Ruth again.

"Oh, sister!" cried Tess.

"Poor, dear Billy Bumps!" exclaimed Dot, with an arm around the short, thick neck of the goat.

"If yo' lets me 'spressify maself," said Uncle Rufus, slowly, "I'd say dat mebbe I could put him in one oh de hen runs. We don't need 'em both jest now."

"Goody!" cried Tess and Dot, clapping their hands. "Let's, Ruthie!"

The older sister's doubts were overborne. She agreed to the proposal, while Agnes said:

"We might as well have a goat. We have a pig 'most every day. That pig of Mr. Con Murphy's is always coming under the fence and tearing up the garden. A goat could do no more harm."

"But we don't want the place a menagerie," objected Ruth.

Dot said, gravely, "Maybe the goat and the pig will play together, and so the pig won't do so much damage."

"The next time that pig comes in here, I'm going right around to Mr. Con Murphy and complain," declared Agnes, with emphasis.

"Oh! we don't want to have trouble with any neighbor," objected Ruth, quickly.

"My! you'd let folks ride right over you," said Agnes, with scorn for Ruth's timidity.

"I don't think that poor cobbler, Mr. Murphy, will ride over me—unless he rides on his pig," laughed Ruth, as she followed Mrs. MacCall indoors.

Tess had an idea and she was frank to express it. "Uncle Rufus, this goat is very strong. Can't you fashion a harness and some kind of a cart for him so that we can take turns riding—Dot and me? He used to draw Sam Pinkney."

"Glo-ree!" grumbled the colored man again. "I kin see where I got my han's full wid disher goat—I do!"

"But you *can*, Uncle Rufus?" said Tess.

"Oh, yes, chile. I s'pect so. But fust off let me git him shut up in de hen-yard, else he'll be eatin' up de hull ob Mis' MacCall's wash—ya'as'm!"

The poultry pens were fenced with strong woven wire, and

one of them was not in use. Into this enclosure Mr. Billy Bumps was led. When the strap was taken off, he made a dive for Uncle Rufus, but the darky was nimble, despite his years.

"Yo' butt me, yo' horned scalawag!" gasped the old colored man, when once safe on the outside of the pen, "an' I won't gib yo' nottin' ter chew on but an old rubber boot fo' de nex' week—dat's what I'll do."

The old Corner House, as the Stower homestead was known to Milton folk, stood facing Main Street, its side yard running back a long way on Willow Street. It was a huge colonial mansion, with big pillars in front, and two wings thrown out behind. For years before the Kenway girls and Aunt Sarah Maltby had come here to live, the premises outside—if not within—had been sadly neglected.

But energetic Ruth Kenway had insisted upon trimming the lawn and hedges, planting a garden, repairing the summer-house, and otherwise making neat the appearance of the dilapidated old place.

On the Main Street side of the estate the property of Mr. Creamer joined the Corner House yard, but the Creamer property did not extend back as far as that of the Stower place. In the corner at the rear the tiny yard of Con Murphy touched the big place. Mr. Murphy was a cobbler, who held title to a small house and garden on a back street.

This man owned a pig—a very friendly pig. Of that pig, more later!

Perhaps it was the fruit that attracted the pig into the Stower yard. The Kenway girls had had plenty of cherries, peaches, apples, pears, and small fruit all through the season. There were still some late peaches ripening, and when Agnes Kenway happened to open her eyes early, the very next morning after the goat came to live with them, she saw the blushing beauty of these peaches through the open window of the ell room she shared with Ruth.

Never had peaches looked so tempting! The tree was a tall seedling, and the upper branches hung their burden near the open window.

All the lower limbs had been stripped by Uncle Rufus. But the old man could not reach these at the top of the tree.

"It will be a mean shame for them to get ripe and fall off," thought Agnes. "I believe I can reach them."

Up she hopped and slipped into her bathrobe. Just enough cool air entered the room to urge her to pull on her hose and slip her feet into slippers.

The window was at the back of the big house, away from the Willow Street side, and well protected from observation (so Agnes thought) by the shrubbery.

Below the window was a narrow ledge which ran around the house under the second story windows. It took the reckless girl but a moment to get out upon this ledge. To tell the truth she had tried this caper before—but never at such an early hour.

Clinging to the window frame, she leaned outward, and grasped with her other hand a laden, limb. The peaches were right before her; but she could not pluck them.

"Oh! if I only had a third hand," cried Agnes, aloud.

Then, recklessly determined to reach the fruit, she let go of the window frame and stretched her hand for the nearest blushing peach. To her horror she found her body swinging out from the side of the house!

Her weight bore against the limb, and pushed it farther and farther away from the house-wall; Agnes' peril was plain and imminent. Unable to seize the window frame again and draw herself back, she was about to fall between the peach tree and the side of the house!

CHAPTER II

THE WHITE-HEADED BOY

"The Corner House Girls," as they had come to be known to Milton folk, and as they are known to the readers of the first volume of this series, had occupied the great mansion opposite the lower end of the Parade Ground, since the spring before.

They had come from Bloomingsburg, where their father and mother had died, leaving them without guardianship. But when Uncle Peter Stower died and left most of his property to his four nieces, Mr. Howbridge, the lawyer, had come for the Kenway sisters and established them in the old Corner House.

Here they had spent the summer getting acquainted with Milton folk (making themselves liked by most of the neighbors), and gradually getting used to their changed circumstances.

For in Bloomingsburg the Kenways had lived among very poor people, and were very poor themselves. Now they were very fortunately conditioned, having a beautiful home, plenty of money to spend (under the direction of Mr. Howbridge) and the opportunity of making many friends.

With them, to the old mansion, had come Aunt Sarah Maltby. Really, she was no relation at all to the Kenway girls, but she had lived with them ever since they could remember.

In her youth Aunt Sarah had lived in the old Corner House, so this seemed like home to her. Uncle Rufus had served the aforetime owner of the place for many years, too; so *he* was at home here. And as for Mrs. MacCall, she had come to help Ruth and her sisters soon after their establishment in the old Corner House, and by this time had grown to be indispensable.

This was the household, saving Sandyface, the cat, and her four kittens—Spotty, Almira, Popocatepetl and Bungle. And now there was the goat, Mr. Billy Bumps.

Ruth was an intellectual looking girl—so people said. She had little color, and her black hair was "stringy"—which she hated! Now that she was no longer obliged to consider the expenditure of each dollar so carefully, the worried look about her big brown eyes, and the compression of her lips, had relaxed. For two years Ruth had been the head of the household and it had made her old before her time.

She was only a girl yet, however; her sixteenth birthday was not long behind her. She liked fun and was glad of the release from much of her former care. And when she laughed, her eyes were brilliant and her mouth surprisingly sweet.

The smaller girls—Tess (nobody ever called her Theresa) and Dorothy—were both pretty and lively. Dot was Ruth in miniature, a little, fairy-like brunette. Tess, who was ten, had a very kind heart and was tactful. She had some of Ruth's dignity and more of Agnes' good looks.

The twelve year old—the fly-away—the irrepressible—what shall we say about her? That she laughed easily, cried stormily, was always playing pranks, rather tomboyish, affectionate—utterly thoughtless—

Well, there is Agnes, out of the bedroom window in her bathrobe and slippers just at dawn, with the birds chirping their first chorus, and not a soul about (so she supposed) to either see or help her in her sudden predicament.

She really was in danger; there was no doubt of it. A scream for help would not bring Ruth in time; and it was doubtful if her older sister could do anything to help her.

"Oh—*oh*—OH!" gasped Agnes, in crescendo. "I—am—go—ing—to—fall!"

And on the instant—the very sweetest sound Agnes Kenway had ever heard (she admitted this fact afterward)—a boy's voice ejaculated:

"No you're not! Hang on for one minute!"

The side gate clicked. Feet scurried across the lawn, and under her as she glanced downward, Agnes saw a slim, white-faced youth appear. He had white hair, too; he was a regular tow-head. He was dressed in a shiny black suit that was at least two full sizes too small for him. The trousers hitched above his shoe-tops and the sleeves of his jacket were so short that they displayed at least four inches of wrist.

Agnes took in these points on the instant—before she could say another word. The boy was a stranger to her; she had never seen him before.

But he went to work just as though he had been introduced!

Grace Brooks Hill

He flung off his cap and stripped off the jacket, too, in a twinkling. It seemed to Agnes as though he climbed up the tree and reached the limb she clung to as quickly as any cat.

He flung up his legs, wound them about the butt of the limb like two black snakes, and seized Agnes' wrists. "Swing free—I've got you!" he commanded.

Agnes actually obeyed. There was something impelling in his voice; but likewise she felt that there was sufficient strength in those hands that grasped her wrists, to hold her.

Her feet slipped from the ledge and she shot down. The white-haired boy swung out, too, but they did not fall as Agnes agonizingly expected, after she had trusted herself to the unknown.

There was some little shock, but not much; their bodies swung clear of the tree—he with his head down, and she with her slippered feet almost touching the wet grass.

"All right?" demanded the white-head. "Let go!"

He dropped her. She stood upright, and unhurt, but swayed a little, weakly. The next instant he was down and stood, breathing quickly, before her.

"Why—why—why!" gasped Agnes. Just like that! "Why, you did that just like a circus."

Oddly enough the white-haired boy scowled and a dusky color came slowly into his naturally pale cheek.

"What do you say that for?" he asked, dropping his gaze, and picking up his cap and jacket. "What do you mean—circus?"

"Why," said Agnes, breathlessly, "just like one of those acrobats that fly over the heads of the people, and do all those curious things in the air—Why! you know."

"How do I know?" demanded the boy, quite fiercely.

It became impressed upon Agnes' mind that the stranger was angry. She did not know why, and she only felt gratitude—and curiosity—toward him.

"Didn't you ever go to a circus?" she asked, slowly.

The boy hesitated. Then he said, bluntly: "No!" and Agnes knew it was the truth, for he looked now unwaveringly into her eyes.

"My! you've missed a lot," she breathed. "So did we till this summer. Then Mr. Howbridge took us to one of those that came to Milton."

"What circus was it you went to?" the boy asked, quickly.

"Aaron Wall's Magnificent Double Show," repeated Agnes, carefully. "There was another came—Twomley & Sorter's Herculean Circus and Menagerie; but we didn't see that one."

The boy listened as though he considered the answer of some importance. At the end he sighed. "No; I never went to a circus," he repeated.

"But you're just wonderful," Agnes declared. "I never saw a boy like you."

"And I never saw a girl like you," returned the white-haired boy, and his quick grin made him look suddenly friendly. "What did you crawl out of that window for?"

"To get a peach."

"Did you get it?"

"No. It was just out of reach, after all. And then I leaned too far."

The boy was looking up quizzically at the high-hung fruit. "If you want it awfully bad?" he suggested.

"There's more than one," said Agnes, giggling. "And you're welcome to all you can pick."

"Do you mean it?" he shot in, at once casting cap and jacket on the ground again.

"Yes. Help yourself. Only toss me down one."

"This isn't a joke, now?" the boy asked. "You've got a *right* to tell me to take 'em?"

"Oh, mercy! Yes!" ejaculated Agnes. "Do you think I'd tell a story?"

"I don't know," he said, bluntly.

"Well! I like *that*!" cried Agnes, with some vexation.

"I don't know you and you don't know me," said the boy. "Everybody that I meet doesn't tell me the truth. So now!"

"Do *you* always tell the truth?" demanded Agnes, shrewdly.

Again the boy flushed, but there was roguishness in his brown eyes. "I don't *dare* tell it—sometimes," he said.

"Well, there's nobody to scare *me* into story-telling," said Agnes, loftily, deciding that she did not like this boy so well, after all.

"Oh, I'll risk it—for the peaches," said the white-haired boy, coming back to the—to him—principal subject of discussion, and immediately he climbed up the tree.

Agnes gasped again. "My goodness!" she thought. "I know Sandyface couldn't go up that tree any quicker—not even with Sam Pinkney's bulldog after her."

He was a slim boy and the limbs scarcely bent under his weight—not even when he was in the top of the tree. He seemed to know just how to balance himself, while standing there, and fearlessly used both hands to pick the remaining fruit.

Two of the biggest, handsomest peaches he dropped, one after the other, into the lap of Agnes' thick bath-gown as she held it up before her. The remainder of the fruit he bestowed about his own person, dropping it through the neck of his shirt until the peaches quite swelled out its fullness all about his waist. His trousers were held in place by a stout strap, instead of by suspenders.

He came down from the tree as easily as he had climbed it—and with the peaches intact.

"They must have a fine gymnasium at the school where you go," said Agnes, admiringly.

"I never went to school," said the boy, and blushed again.

Agnes was very curious. She had already established herself on the porch step, wrapped the robe closely around her, shook her two plaits back over her shoulders, and now sunk her teeth into the first peach. With her other hand she beckoned the white-haired boy to sit down beside her.

"Come and eat them," she said. "Breakfast won't be ready for ever and ever so long yet."

The boy removed the peaches he had picked, and made a little pyramid of them on the step. Then he put on his jacket and cap before he accepted her invitation. Meanwhile Agnes was eating the peach and contemplating him gravely.

She had to admit, now that she more closely inspected them, that the white-haired boy's garments were extremely shabby. Jacket and trousers were too small for him, as she had previously observed. His shirt was faded, very clean, and the elbows were patched. His shoes were broken, but polished brightly.

When he bit into the first peach his eye brightened and he ate the fruit greedily. Agnes believed he must be very hungry, and for once the next-to-the-oldest Kenway girl showed some tact.

"Will you stay to breakfast with us?" she asked. "Mrs. MacCall always gets up at six o'clock. And Ruth will want to see you, too. Ruth's the oldest of us Kenways."

"Is this a boarding-house?" asked the boy, seriously.

"Oh, no!"

"It's big enough."

"I 'spect it is," said Agnes. "There are lots of rooms we never use."

"Could—could a feller get to stay here?" queried the white-haired boy.

"Oh! I don't know," gasped Agnes. "You—you'd have to ask Ruth. And Mr. Howbridge, perhaps."

"Who's he?" asked the boy, suspiciously.

"Our lawyer."

"Does he live here?"

"Oh, no. There isn't any man here but Uncle Rufus. He's a colored man who lived with Uncle Peter who used to own this house. Uncle Peter gave it to us Kenway girls when he died."

"Oh! then you own it?" asked the boy.

"Mr. Howbridge is the executor of the estate; but we four Kenway girls—and Aunt Sarah—have the income from it. And we came to live in this old Corner House almost as soon as Uncle Peter Stower died."

"Then you could take boarders if you wanted to?" demanded the white-haired boy, sticking to his proposition like a leech.

"Why—maybe—I'd ask Ruth—"

"I'd pay my way," said the boy, sharply, and flushing again. She could see that he was a very proud boy, in spite of his evident poverty.

"I've got some money saved. I'd earn more—after school. I'm going to school across the Parade Ground there—when it opens. I've already seen the superintendent of schools. He says I belong in the highest grammar grade."

"Why!" cried Agnes, "that's the grade *I* am going into."

"I'm older than you are," said the boy, with that quick, angry flush mounting into his cheeks. "I'm fifteen. But I never had a chance to go to school."

"That is too bad," said Agnes, sympathetically. She saw that he was eager to enter school and sympathized with him on that point, for she was eager herself.

"We'll have an awfully nice teacher," she told him. "Miss Shipman."

Just then Ruth appeared at the upper window and looked down upon them.

CHAPTER III

THE PIG IS IMPORTANT

"My goodness! what are you doing down there, Aggie?" demanded Ruth. "And who's that with you!"

"I—I got up to get a peach, Ruthie," explained Agnes, rather stammeringly. "And I asked the boy to have one, too."

Ruth, looking out of the bedroom window, expressed her amazement at this statement by a long, blank stare at her sister and the white-haired boy. Agnes felt that there was further explanation due from her.

"You see," she said, "he—he just saved my life—perhaps."

"How is that?" gasped Ruth. "Were you going to eat *all* those peaches by yourself! They might have killed you, that's a fact."

"No, no!" cried Agnes, while the boy's face flushed up darkly again. "He saved me from falling out of the tree."

"Out of the tree? *This* tree!" demanded Ruth. "How did you get into it?"

"From—from the window."

"Goodness! you never! And with your bathrobe on!" ejaculated Ruth, her eyes opening wider.

As an "explainer," Agnes was deficient. But she tried to start the story all over again. "Hush!" commanded Ruth, suddenly. "Wait till I come down. We'll have everybody in the house awake, and it is too early."

She disappeared and the boy looked doubtfully at Agnes. "Is she the oldest sister you spoke of?"

"Yes. That's Ruth."

"She's kind of bossy, isn't she?"

"Oh! but we like to be bossed by Ruthie. She's just like mother was to us," declared Agnes.

"I shouldn't think you'd like it," growled the white-haired boy. "I hate to be bossed—and I won't be, either!"

"You have to mind in school," said Agnes, slowly.

"That's another thing," said the boy. "But I wouldn't let another boy boss me."

In five minutes Ruth was down upon the back porch, too. She was neat and fresh and smiling. When Ruth smiled, dimples came at the corners of her mouth and the laughter jumped right out of her eyes at you in a most unexpected way. The white-haired boy evidently approved of her, now that he saw her close to.

"Tell me how it happened!" commanded Ruth of her sister,

and Agnes did so. In the telling the boy lost nothing of courage and dexterity, you may be sure!

"Why, that's quite wonderful!" cried Ruth, smiling again at the boy. "It was awfully rash of you, Aggie, but it was providential this—this—You haven't told me his name?"

"Why! I don't know it myself," confessed Agnes.

"And after all he did for you!" exclaimed Ruth, in admonition.

"Aw—it wasn't anything," growled the boy, with all the sex's objection to being thought a hero.

"You must be very strong—a regular athlete," declared Ruth.

"Any other boy could do it."

"No!"

"If he knew how," limited the white-haired boy.

"And how did you learn so much!" asked Ruth, curiously.

Again the red flushed into his pale face. "Practicin'. That's all," he said, rather doggedly.

"Won't you tell us who you are?" asked Ruth, feeling that the boy was keeping up a wall between them.

"Neale O'Neil."

"Do you live in Milton?"

"I do now."

"But I never remember seeing you before," Ruth said, puzzled.

"I only came to stay yesterday," confessed the boy, and once more he grinned and his eyes were roguish.

"Oh! then your folks have just moved in?"

"I haven't any folks."

"No family at all?"

"No, ma'am," said Neale O'Neil, rather sullenly Ruth thought

"You are not all alone—a boy like you?"

"Why not?" demanded he, tartly. "I'm 'most as old as you are."

"But *I* am not all alone," said Ruth, pleasantly. "I have the girls—my sisters; and I have Aunt Sarah—and Mr. Howbridge."

"Well, I haven't anybody," confessed Neale O'Neil, rather gloomily.

"You surely have some friends?" asked Ruth, not only curious, but sympathetic.

"Not here. I'm alone, I tell you." Yet he did not speak so ungratefully now. It was impressed upon his mind that Ruth's questions were friendly. "And I am going to school here. I've got some money saved up. I want to find a boarding place where I can part pay my board, perhaps, by working around. I can do lots of things."

"I see. Look after furnaces, and clean up yards, and all that?"

"Yes," said the boy, with heightened interest. "This other one—your sister—says you have plenty of empty rooms in this big house. Would you take a boarder?"

"Goodness me! I never thought of such a thing."

"You took in that Mrs. Treble and Double Trouble," whispered Agnes, who rather favored the suit of the white-haired boy.

"They weren't boarders," Ruth breathed.

"No. But you could let him come just as well." To tell the truth, Agnes had always thought that "a boy around the house would be awfully handy"—and had often so expressed herself. Dot had agreed with her, while Ruth and Tess held boys in general in much disfavor.

Neale O'Neil had stood aside, not listening, but well aware that the sisters were discussing his suggestion. Finally he flung in: "I ain't afraid to work. And I'm stronger than I look."

"You *must* be strong, Neale," agreed Ruth, warmly, "if you did what Aggie says you did. But we have Uncle Rufus, and he does most everything, though he's old. I don't just know what to say to you."

At that moment the sound of a sash flung up at the other side of the ell startled the three young folk. Mrs. MacCall's voice sounded sharply on the morning air:

"That pig! in that garden again! Shoo! Shoo, you beast! I wish you'd eat yourself to death and then maybe your master would keep you home!"

"Oh, oh, oh!" squealed Agnes. "Con Murphy's pig after our cabbages!"

"That pig again?" echoed Ruth, starting after the flying Agnes.

The latter forgot how lightly she was shod, and before she was half-way across the lawn her feet and ankles were saturated with dew.

"You'll get sopping wet, Aggie!" cried Ruth, seeing the bed slippers flopping, half off her sister's feet.

"Can't help it now," stammered Agnes. "Got to get that pig! Oh, Ruth! the hateful thing!"

The cobbler's porker was a freebooter of wide experience. The old Corner House yard was not the only forbidden premises he roved in. He always dug a new hole under the fence at night, and appeared early in the morning, roving at will among the late vegetables in Ruth's garden.

He gave a challenging grunt when he heard the girls, raised his head, and his eyes seemed fairly to twinkle as he saw their wild attack. A cabbage leaf hung crosswise in his jaws and he continued to champ upon it reflectively as he watched the enemy.

"Shoo! Shoo!" shouted Agnes.

"That pig is possessed," moaned Ruth. "He's taken the very one I was going to have Uncle Rufus cut for our Saturday's dinner."

Seeing that the charging column numbered but two girls, the pig tossed his head, uttered a scornful grunt, and started slowly out of the garden. He was in no hurry. He had grown fat on these raids, and he did not propose to lose any of the avoirdupois thus gained, by hurrying.

Leisurely he advanced toward the boundary fence. There was the fresh earth where he had rooted out of Mr. Con Murphy's yard into this larger and freer range.

Suddenly, to his piggish amazement, another figure—a swiftly flying figure—got between him and his way of escape. The pig stopped, snorted, threw up his head—and instantly lost all his calmness of mind.

"Oh, that boy!" gasped Ruth.

Neale O'Neil was in the pig's path, and he bore a stout fence-picket. For the first time in his experience in raiding these particular premises, his pigship had met with a foe worthy of his attention. Four girls, an old lady, and an ancient colored retainer, in giving chase heretofore, merely lent spice to the pig's buccaneering ventures.

He dashed forward with a sudden grunt, but the slim boy did not dodge. Instead he brought that picket down with emphasis upon the pig's snout.

"Wee! wee! wee!" shrieked the pig, and dashed headlong down the yard, blind to anything but pain and immediate escape.

"Oh! don't hurt him!" begged Ruth.

But Agnes had caught her sister around the neck and was hanging upon her, weak with laughter. "Did you hear him?

Did you hear him?" she gasped. "He's French, and all the time I thought he was Irish. Did you hear how plain he said 'Yes,' with a pure Parisian accent?"

"Oh, Neale!" cried Ruth again. "Don't hurt him!"

"No; but I'll scare him so he won't want to come in here again in a hurry," declared the boy.

"Let the boy alone, Ruth," gasped Agnes. "I have no sympathy for the pig."

The latter must have felt that everybody was against him. He could look nowhere in the enemy's camp for sympathy. He dove several times at the fence, but every old avenue of escape had been closed. And that boy with the picket was between him and the hole by which he had entered.

Finally he headed for the hen runs. There was a place in the fence of the farther yard where Uncle Rufus had been used to putting a trough of feed for the poultry. The empty trough was still there, but when the pig collided with it, it shot into the middle of the apparently empty yard. The pig followed it, scrouging under the fence, and squealing intermittently.

"There!" exclaimed Neale O'Neil. "Why not keep him in that yard and make his owner pay to get him home again?"

"Oh! I couldn't ask poor Mr. Murphy for money," said Ruth, giving an anxious glance at the little cottage over the fence. She expected every moment to hear the cobbler coming to the rescue of his pet.

And the pig did not propose to remain impounded. He dashed to the boundary fence and found an aperture. Through it he caught a glimpse of home and safety.

But the hole was not quite deep enough. Head and shoulders went through all right; but there his pigship stuck.

There was a scurrying across the cobbler's yard, but the Kenway girls and their new friend did not hear this. Instead, they were startled by a sudden rattling of hoofs in a big drygoods box that stood inside the poultry pen.

"What's that?" demanded Neale O'Neil.

"It's—it's Billy Bumps!" shrieked Agnes.

Out of the box dashed the goat. The opening fronted the boundary fence, beneath which the pig was stuck. Perhaps Billy Bumps took the rapidly curling and uncurling tail of the pig for a challenging banner. However that might be, he lowered his head and catapulted himself across the yard as true as a bullet for the target.

Slam! the goat landed just where it seemed to do the most good, for the remainder of the pig shot through the aperture in the board fence on the instant. One more affrighted squeal the pig uttered, and then:

"Begorra! 'Tis ivry last brith in me body ye've knocked out," came from the other side of the fence.

"Oh, Agnes!" gasped Ruth, as the sisters clung together, weak from laughter. "That pig can't be French after all; for that's as broad an Irish brogue as ever I heard!"

CHAPTER IV

NEALE O'NEIL GETS ESTABLISHED

Perhaps Billy Bumps was as much amazed as anybody when he heard what sccmcd to be the pig expressing his dissatisfaction in a broad Irish brogue on the other side of the fence.

The old goat's expression was indeed comical. He backed away from the hole through which he had just shot the raider head-first, shook his own head, stamped, and seemed to listen intently to the hostile language.

"Be th' powers! 'Tis a dirthy, mane thrick, so ut is! An' th' poor pig kem t'roo th' hole like it was shot out of a gun."

"It's Mr. Murphy!" whispered Ruth, almost as much overcome with laughter as Agnes herself.

Neale O'Neil was frankly amazed; but in a moment he, like the girls, jumped to the right conclusion. The cobbler had run to the rescue of his pet. He had seized it by the ears as it was trying to crowd under the fence, and tugged, too. When old Billy Bumps had released his pigship, the latter had bowled the cobbler over.

Mr. Con Murphy possessed a vocabulary of most forceful

and picturesque words, well colored with the brogue he had brought on his tongue from "the ould dart." Mr. Murphy's "Irish was up" and when he got his breath, which the pig had well nigh knocked out of him, the little old cobbler gave his unrestrained opinion of the power that had shot the pig under the fence.

Ruth could not allow the occurrence to end without an explanation. She ran to the fence and peered over.

"Oh, Mr. Murphy!" she cried. "You're not really hurt?"

"For the love av mercy!" ejaculated the cobbler. "Niver tell me that *youse* was the one that pushed the pig through the fince that har-rd that he kem near flyin' down me t'roat? Ye niver could have done it, Miss Kenway—don't be tillin' me. Is it wan o' thim big Jarmyn guns youse have got in there, that the pa-apers do be tillin' erbout?"

He was a comical looking old fellow at best, and out here at this early hour, with only his trousers slipped on over his calico nightshirt, and heelless slippers on his feet, he cut a curious figure indeed.

Mr. Con Murphy was a red-faced man, with a fringe of sandy whiskers all around his countenance like a frame, having his lips, chin and cheeks smoothly shaven. He had no family, lived alone in the cottage, and worked very hard at his cobbler's bench.

"Why, Mr. Murphy!" cried Ruth. "Of course *I* didn't push your pig through the fence."

"It was Billy Bumps," giggled Agnes.

"Who is that, thin?" demanded Mr. Murphy, glaring at Neale

O'Neil. "That young felley standin' there, I dunno?"

"No. I only cracked your pig over the nose with this fence paling," said the boy. "I wonder you don't keep the pig at home."

"Oh, ye do, do ye?" cried the little Irishman. "Would ye have me lock him into me spare bedroom?"

"I would if he were mine—before I'd let him be a nuisance to the neighbors," declared Neale O'Neil.

"Oh, Neale!" interposed Ruth. "You mustn't speak so. Of course the pig is annoying—"

"He's a nuisance. Anybody can see that," said the boy, frankly.

"'Tis a smart lad ye ar-re," sneered Mr. Murphy. "Show me how ter kape the baste at home. The fince is not mine, whativer ye say. If it isn't strong enough to kape me pig out—"

"I'll fix it for you in half a day—if you'll pay me for it," interrupted Neale O'Neil.

"How will ye do ut? and how much will ye tax me?" queried the cautious cobbler.

"I'd string a strand of barbed wire all along the bottom of the fence. That will stop the pig from rooting, I'll be bound."

The old Irishman rubbed his chin reflectively. "'Twill cost a pretty penny," he said.

"Then," said Neale O'Neil, winking at the girls, "let's turn

Billy Bumps loose, and the next time the pig comes in I hope he'll butt his head off!"

"Hi!" shouted Mr. Murphy. "Who's this Billy Bumps ye air talkin' so fast about?"

"That's our goat," explained Agnes, giggling.

Mr. Murphy's roving eyes caught sight of the billy, just then reflectively nibbling an old shoe that had been flung into the pen.

"Is that the baste that shot me pig under the fince?" he yelped.

Billy Bumps raised his head, shook his venerable beard, and blatted at the cobbler.

"He admits the accusation," chuckled Agnes.

"Shure," said Mr. Murphy, wagging his head, "if that thunderin' ould pi-*rat* of a goat ever gits a *good* whack at me pig, he'd dr-rive him through a knothole! Kem over and see me by and by, la-a-ad," he added, to Neale, his eyes twinkling, "and we'll bargain about that barbed wire job."

"I'll be over to see you, sir," promised the white-haired boy.

For Ruth had nudged his elbow and whispered: "You must stay to breakfast with us, Neale."

The boy did so; but he successfully kept up that wall between the girls' curiosity and his own private history. He frankly admitted that he had gone hungry of late to save the little sum he had hoarded for the opening of the Milton schools.

"For I'll have to buy some books—the superintendent told me so. And I won't have so much time then to earn money for my keep," he said. "But I am going to school whether I eat regularly, or not. I never had a chance before."

"To eat?" asked Agnes, slily.

"Not like this!" declared Neale, laughing, as he looked about the abundant table.

But without asking him point-blank just what his life had been, and why he had never been to school, Ruth did not see how she was to learn more than the white-haired boy wished to tell them.

The girls all liked him. Of course, Aunt Sarah, who was very odd, when she came to table did not speak to the boy, and she glared at him whenever he helped himself to one of Mrs. MacCall's light biscuit. But the housekeeper appreciated the compliment he gave her cooking.

"I guess I don't make such bad biscuit after all," she said. "Sometimes you girls eat so little at breakfast that I've thought my days for hot bread making were over."

Neale blushed and stopped eating almost at once. Although frank to admit his poverty, he did not like to make a display of his appetite.

Ruth had been thinking seriously of the proposition, and after breakfast she told Neale that he might remain at the old Corner House—and welcome—until he found just the place he desired.

"But I must pay you," said the boy, earnestly.

"We don't really need to be paid, Neale," said Ruth, warmly. "There are so many empty rooms here, you know—and there is always enough for one more at our table."

"I couldn't stop if I didn't do something to pay you," Neale said, bluntly. "I'm no beggar."

"I tell you!" Ruth cried, having a happy thought. "You can help us clean house. We must get it all done before school begins, so as to help Mrs. MacCall. Uncle Rufus can't beat rugs, and lift and carry, like a younger person."

"I'll do anything," promised Neale O'Neil. "But first I'll fix that Irishman's fence so his pig can't root into your yard any more."

He was over at the cobbler's most of the day, but he showed up for the noon dinner. Ruth had made him promise to come when he was called.

Mrs. MacCall insisted upon heaping his plate with the hearty food. "Don't tell *me*," she said. "A boy's always hollow clean down to his heels—and you're pretty tall for your age. It'll take some time to fill you up properly."

"If I just let myself go, I really *can* eat," admitted Neale O'Neil. "And this is so much better cooking than I have been used to."

There it was again! Ruth and Agnes wanted—oh! *so* much— to ask him where he had lived, and with whom, that he had never before had proper food given him. But although Neale was jolly, and free to speak about everything else, the moment anything was suggested that might lead to his explaining his previous existence, he shied just like an unbroken colt.

"Just as if he didn't *have* any existence at all," complained Agnes, "before he ran through our side gate this morning, yelling to me to 'hold on.'"

"Never mind. We will win his confidence in time," Ruth said, in her old-fashioned way.

"Even if he had done something—"

"Hush!" commanded Ruth. "Suppose somebody should hear? The children for instance."

"Well! of course we don't really know anything about him."

"And I am sure he has not done anything very bad. He may be ashamed of his former life, but I am sure it is not because of his own fault. He is just very proud and, I think, very ambitious."

Of the last there could be no doubt. Neale O'Neil was not content to remain idle at all. As soon as he had finished at Mr. Murphy's, he returned to the old Corner House and beat rugs until it was time for supper.

There was little wonder that his appetite seemed to increase rather than diminish—he worked so hard!

"I don't believe you ever *did* have enough to eat," giggled Agnes.

"I don't know that I ever did," admitted Neale.

"Suppose you should wake up in the night?" she suggested. "If you were real hungry it would be dreadful. I think you'd better take some crackers and cheese upstairs with, you when you go to bed."

Neale took this all in good temper, but Mrs. MacCall exclaimed, suddenly:

"There! I knew there was something I forgot from the store to-day. Tess, do you and Dot want to run over to Mr. Stetson's after supper and bring me some crackers?"

"Of course we will, Mrs. MacCall," replied Tess.

"And I'll take my Alice-doll. She needs an airing," declared Dot. "Her health isn't all that we might wish since that Lillie Treble buried her alive."

"Buried her alive?" cried Neale. "Playing savages?"

"No," said Tess, gravely. "And she buried dried apples with her, too. It was an awful thing, and we don't talk about it— much," she added, in a whisper, with a nod toward Dot's serious face.

Out of this trip to the grocery arose a misunderstanding that was very funny in the end. Ruth had chosen the very room, at the back of the house, in which the lady from Ipsilanti and her little daughter had slept, for the use of Neale O'Neil. After supper she had gone up there to make the bed afresh, and she was there when Tess and Dorothy returned home from the store, filled to the lips, and bursting, with a wonderful piece of news.

"Oh, dear me, Ruthie!" cried Dot, being the leader, although her legs were not the longest. "Did you know we all have to be 'scalloped before we can go to school here in Milton?"

"Be *what*?" gasped the oldest Kenway girl, smoothing up the coverlet of the bed and preparing to plump the pillows.

"No," panted Tess, putting her bundle on the stand by the head of the bed. "'Tisn't 'scalloped, Tess. It's vac—vacilation, I believe. Anyway, it's some operation, and we all have to have it."

"Goodness me!" exclaimed Ruth, laughing. "We've all been vaccinated, kiddies—and it wasn't such a dreadful operation, after all. All we'll have to do is to show our arms to the doctor and he'll see we were vaccinated recently."

"Well!" said Dot. "I knew it had something to do with that 'scallop mark on my arm," and she tried to roll up the sleeve of her frock to see the small but perfect scar that was the result of her vaccination.

They all left the room, laughing. Two hours later the house quieted down, for the family had retired to their several rooms.

To Neale O'Neil, the waif, the big house was a very wonderful place. The fine old furniture, the silver plate of which Uncle Rufus took such loving care, the happy, merry girls, benevolent Mrs. MacCall and her odd sayings, even Aunt Sarah with her grim manner, seemed creatures and things of another world. For the white-haired boy had lived, since he could remember, an existence as far removed from this quiet home-life at the old Corner House, as could be imagined!

He told Agnes laughingly that he would be afraid to leave his room during the night, for fear of getting lost in the winding passages, and up and down the unexpected flights of stairs at the back of the house.

He heard the girls go away laughing when they had showed him to his room. There was a gas-jet burning and he turned it up the better to see the big apartment.

"Hullo! what's this?" Neale demanded, as he spied a paper bag upon the stand.

He crossed to the head of the bed, and put his hand on the package. There was no mistaking the contents of the bag at first touch.

Crackers!

"That's the fat girl!" exclaimed Neale, and for a moment he was really a little angry with Agnes.

It was true, he *had* gorged himself on Mrs. MacCall's good things. She had urged him so, and he had really been on "short commons" for several days. Agnes had suggested his taking crackers and cheese to bed with him—and here was a whole bag of crackers!

He sat down a moment and glowered at the package. For one thing, he was tempted to put on his cap and jacket and leave the Corner House at once.

But that would be childish. And Ruth had been so kind to him. He was sure the oldest Kenway girl would never perpetrate such a joke.

"Of course, Aggie didn't mean to be unkind," he thought, at last, his good judgment coming to his rescue. "I—I'd like to pay her back. I—I will!"

He jumped up and went to the door, carrying the bag of crackers with him. He opened the door and listened. Somewhere, far away, was the sound of muffled laughter.

"I bet that's that Aggie girl!" he muttered, "and she's laughing at me."

CHAPTER V

CRACKERS—AND A TOOTHACHE

The arc light at the corner of Main Street vied with a faint moon in illuminating the passages and corridors of the old Corner House. Deep shadows lay in certain corners and at turns in the halls and staircases; but Neale O'Neil was not afraid of the dark.

The distant laughter spurred him to find the girls' room. He wanted to get square with Agnes, whom he believed had put the bag of crackers beside his bed.

But suddenly a door slammed, and then there was a great silence over the house. From the outside Neale could easily have identified the girls' room. He had seen Aggie climb out of one of the windows of the chamber in question that very morning.

But in a couple of minutes he had to acknowledge that he was completely turned about in this house. He did not know that he had been put to sleep in another wing from that in which the girls' rooms were situated. Only Uncle Rufus slept in this wing besides himself, and he in another story higher.

The white-haired boy came finally to the corridor leading to the main staircase. This was more brilliantly lighted by the electric lamp on the street. He stepped lightly forward and saw a faint light from a transom over one of the front room doors.

"That's where those girls sleep, I bet!" whispered Neale to himself.

The transom was open. There was a little rustling sound within. Then the light went out.

Neale broke the string and opened the bag of crackers. They were of the thick, hard variety known in New England as "Boston" crackers. He took out one and weighed it in his hand. It made a very proper missile.

With a single jerk of his arm he scaled the cracker through the open transom. There was a slight scuffle within, following the cracker's fall.

He paused a moment and then threw a second and a third. Each time the rustling was repeated, and Neale kept up the bombardment believing that, although the girls did not speak, the shower of crackers was falling upon the guilty.

One after the other he flung the crackers through the transom until they were all discharged. Not a sound now from the bombarded quarters. Chuckling, Neale stole away, sure that he would have a big laugh on Agnes in the morning.

But before he got back into his wing of the house, he spied a candle with a girl in a pink kimono behind it.

"Whatever do you want out here, Neale O'Neil? A drink?"

It was Ruth. Neale was full of tickle over his joke, and he

had to relate it.

"I've just been paying off that smart sister of yours in her own coin," he chuckled.

"Which smart sister?"

"Why, Agnes."

"But how?"

Neale told her how he had found the bag of crackers on the table beside his bed. "Nobody but Aggie would be up to such a trick, I know," chuckled Neale. "So I just pitched 'em all through the transom at her."

"What transom?" gasped Ruth, in dismay. "Where did you throw them?"

"Why, right through *that* one," and Neale pointed. "Isn't that the room you and Aggie occupy?"

"My goodness' sakes alive!" cried Ruth, awe-struck. "What *have* you done, Neale O'Neil? *That's Aunt Sarah's room.*"

Ruth rushed to the door, tried it, found it unbolted, and ran in. Her candle but dimly revealed the apartment; but it gave light enough to show that Aunt Sarah was not in evidence.

Almost in the middle of the room stood the big "four-poster," with canopy and counterpane, the fringe of which reached almost to the rag carpet that covered the floor. A cracker crunched under Ruth's slipper-shod foot. Indeed, crackers were everywhere! No part of the room—save beneath the bed itself—had escaped the bombardment.

"Mercy on us!" gasped Ruth, and ran to the bed. She lifted a corner of the counterpane and peered under. A pair of bare heels were revealed and beyond them—supposedly—was the remainder of Aunt Sarah!

"Aunt Sarah! Aunt Sarah! do come out," begged Ruth.

"The ceilin's fallin', Niece Ruth," croaked the old lady. "This rickety old shebang is a-fallin' to pieces at last. I allus told your Uncle Peter it would."

"No, no, Aunt Sarah, it's all right!" cried Ruth. Then she remembered Neale and knew if she told the story bluntly, Aunt Sarah would never forgive the boy.

"Do, *do* come out," she begged, meanwhile scrambling about, herself, to pick up the crackers. She collected most of them that were whole easily enough. But some had broken and the pieces had scattered far and wide.

With some difficulty the old lady crept out from under the far side of the bed. She was ready to retire, her nightcap securely tied under her chin, and all.

When Ruth, much troubled by a desire to laugh, asked her, she explained that the first missile had landed upon her head while she was kneeling beside the bed at her devotions.

"I got up and another of the things hit me on the ear," pursued Aunt Sarah, short and sharp. "Another landed in the small of my back, and I went over into that corner. But pieces of the ceiling were droppin' all over and no matter where I got to, they hit me. So I dove under the bed—"

"Oh! you poor, dear Auntie!"

"If the dratted ceilin's all comin' down, this ain't no place for us to stay," quoth Aunt Sarah.

"I am sure it is all over," urged Ruth. "But if you'd like to go to another room—?"

"And sleep in a bed that ain't been aired in a dog's age?" snapped Aunt Sarah. "I guess not."

"Then, will you come and sleep with me? Aggie can go into the children's room."

"No. If you are sure there ain't no more goin' to fall?"

"I am positive, Auntie."

"Then I'm going to bed," declared the old lady. "But I allus told Peter this old place was bound to go to rack and ruin because o' his miserliness."

Ruth waited till her aunt got into bed, where she almost at once fell asleep. Then the girl scrambled for the remainder of the broken crackers and carried them all out into the hall in the trash basket.

Neale O'Neil was sitting on the top step of the front stairs, waiting for her appearance.

"Well! I guess I did it that time," he said. "She looked at me savage enough to bite, at supper. What's she going to do now—have me arrested and hung?" and he grinned suddenly.

"Oh, Neale!" gasped Ruth, overcome with laughter. "How could you?"

"I thought you girls were in there. I was giving Aggie her

crackers back," Neale grunted.

Ruth explained to him how the crackers had come to be left in his room. Agnes had had nothing to do with it. "I guess the joke is on you, after all, Neale," she said, obliged to laugh in the end.

"Or on that terrible old lady."

"But she doesn't know it is a joke. I don't know what she'll say to-morrow when she sees that none of the ceiling has fallen."

Fortunately Aunt Sarah supplied an explanation herself—and nothing could have shaken her belief in her own opinion. One of her windows was dropped down half way from the top. She was sure that some "rascally boy" outside (she glared at Neale O'Neil when she said it at the breakfast table) had thrown crackers through the window. She had found some of the crumbs.

"And I'll ketch him some day, and then—" She shook her head grimly and relapsed into her accustomed silence.

So Neale did not have to confess his fault and try to make peace with Aunt Sarah. It would have been impossible for him to do this last, Ruth was sure.

But the story of the bag of crackers delighted Agnes. She teased Neale about it unmercifully, and he showed himself to be better-natured and more patient, than Ruth had at first supposed him to be.

The next few days following the appearance of Neale O'Neil at the old Corner House were busy ones indeed. School would open the next week and there was lots to do before that important event.

Brooms searched out dust, long-handled brushes searched out cobwebs, and the first and second floors of the old Corner House were subjected to a thorough renovation.

Above that the girls and Mrs. MacCall decided not to go. The third floor rooms were scarcely ever entered, save by Sandyface and her kittens in search of mice. As for the great garret that ran the full width of the front of the house, *that* had been cleaned so recently (at the time of the "Ghost Party," which is told of in the first volume of this series) that there was no necessity of mounting so high.

The stranger boy who had come to the old Corner House so opportunely, proved himself of inestimable value in the work in hand. Uncle Rufus was saved many a groan by that lively youth, and Mrs. MacCall and the girls pronounced him a valuable assistant.

The young folk were resting on the back porch on Thursday afternoon, chattering like magpies, when suddenly Neale O'Neil spied a splotch of brilliant color coming along Willow Street.

"What do you call this?" demanded he. "Is it a locomotive headlight?"

"Oh! what a ribbon!" gasped Agnes.

"I declare!" said Tess, in her old-fashioned way. "That is Alfredia Blossom. And what a great bow of ribbon she has tied on her head. It's big enough for a sash, Dot."

"Looks like a house afire," commented Neale again.

By this time Alfredia's smiling face was recognizable under the flaming red bow, and Ruth explained:

"She is one of Uncle Rufus' grand-daughters. Her mother, Petunia Blossom, washes for us, and Alfredia is dragging home the wash in that little wagon."

The ribbon, Alfredia wore was at least four inches wide and it was tied in front at the roots of her kinky hair into a bow, the wings of which stuck out on each side like a pair of elephant ears.

The little colored girl came in at the side gate, drawing the wash-basket after her.

"How-do, Miss Ruthie—and Miss Aggie? How-do, Tessie and Dottie? You-all gwine to school on Monday?"

"All of us are going, Alfredia," proclaimed Tess. "Are you going?"

"Mammy done said I could," said Alfredia, rolling her eyes. "But I dunno fo' sho'."

"Why don't you know?" asked Agnes, the curious.

"Dunno as I got propah clo'es to wear, honey. Got ter look mighty fetchin' ter go ter school—ya-as'm!"

"Is that why you've got that great bow on your head?" giggled Agnes. "To make you look 'fetching'?"

"Naw'm. I put dat ol' red sash-bow up dar to 'tract 'tention."

"To attract attention?" repeated Ruth. "Why do you want to attract attention?"

Grace Brooks Hill

"I don't *wanter*, Miss Ruthie."

"Then why do you wear it?"

"So folkses will look at my haid."

Agnes and Neale were vastly amused, but Ruth pursued her inquiry. She wished to get to the bottom of the mystery:

"Why do you want folks to look at your head, Alfredia?"

"So dey won't look at my feet. I done got holes in my shoes—an' dey is Mammy's shoes, anyway. Do you 'spects I kin git by wid 'em on Monday—for dey's de on'iest shoes I got ter wear?"

The Kenways laughed—they couldn't help it. But Ruth did not let the colored girl go away without a pair of half-worn footwear of Agnes' that came somewhere near fitting Alfredia.

"It's just so nice to have so many things that we can afford to give some away," sighed Agnes. "My! my! but we ought to be four happy girls."

One of the Corner House girls was far from happy the next day. Dot came down to breakfast with a most woebegone face, and tenderly caressing her jaw. She had a toothache, and a plate of mush satisfied her completely at the table.

"I—I can't che-e-e-ew!" she wailed, when she tried a bit of toast.

"I am ashamed of you, Dot," said Tess, earnestly. "That tooth is just a little wabbly one, and you ought to have it pulled."

"Ow! don't you touch it!" shrieked Dot.

"I'm not going to," said Tess. "I was reaching for some more butter for my toast—not for your tooth."

"We-ell!" confessed the smallest Kenway; "it just *jumps* when anybody comes toward it."

"Be a brave little girl and go with sister to the dentist," begged Ruth.

"No—please—Ruthie! I can't," wailed Dot.

"Let sister tie a stout thread around it, and you pull it out yourself," suggested Ruth, as a last resort.

Finally Dot agreed to this. That is, she agreed to have the thread tied on. Neale climbed the back fence into Mr. Murphy's premises and obtained a waxed-end of the cobbler. This, he said, would not slip, and Ruth managed to fasten the thread to the root of the little tooth.

"One good jerk, and it's all over!" proclaimed Agnes.

But this seemed horrible to Dot. The tender little gum was sore, and the nerve telegraphed a sense of acute pain to Dot's mind whenever she touched the tooth. One good jerk, indeed!

"I tell you what to do," said Neale to the little girl. "You tie the other end of that waxed-end to a doorknob, and sit down and wait. Somebody will come through the door after a while and jerk the tooth right out!"

"Oh!" gasped Dot.

"Go ahead and try it, Dot," urged Agnes. "I'm afraid you are a little coward."

This accusation from her favorite sister made Dot feel very badly. She betook herself to another part of the house, the black thread hanging from her lips.

"What door are you going to sit behind, Dot?" whispered Tess. "I'll come and do it—*just as easy!*"

"No, you sha'n't!" cried Dot. "You sha'n't know. And I don't want to know who is going to j-j-jerk it out," and she ran away, sobbing.

Being so busy that morning, the others really forgot the little girl. None of them saw her take a hassock, put it behind the sitting-room door that was seldom opened, and after tying the string to the knob, seat herself upon the hassock and wait for something to happen.

She waited. Nobody came near that room. The sun shone warmly in at the windows, the bees buzzed, and Dot grew drowsy. Finally she fell fast asleep with her tooth tied to the doorknob.

CHAPTER VI

AGNES LOSES HER TEMPER AND DOT HER TOOTH

It was on this morning—Friday, ever a fateful day according to the superstitiously inclined—that the incident of the newspaper advertisement arose.

The paper boy had very early thrown the Kenways' copy of the Milton *Morning Post* upon the front veranda. Aunt Sarah spent part of each forenoon reading that gossipy sheet. She insisted upon seeing the paper just as regularly as she insisted upon having her five cents' worth of peppermint-drops to take to church in her pocket on Sunday morning.

But on this particular morning she did not take the paper in before going to her room after breakfast, and Neale strolled out and picked up the sheet.

Ruth was behind him, but he did not know of her presence. She had been about to secure the morning paper and run upstairs with it, to save Aunt Sarah the bother of coming down again. As she was about to ask the boy for it, Ruth noticed that he was staring rigidly at the still folded paper. His eyes were fixed upon something that appeared in the very first column of the *Post*.

Now, the *Morning Post* devoted the first column of its front page to important announcements and small advertisements— like "Lost and Found," the death and marriage notices, and "personals." Agnes called it the "Agony Column," for the "personals" always headed it.

Ruth was sure Neale was staring at something printed very near the top of the column. He stood there, motionless, long enough to have read any ordinary advertisement half a dozen times.

Then he laid the paper quietly on one of the porch chairs and tiptoed off the veranda, disappearing around the corner of the house without looking back once; so Ruth did not see his face.

"What can be the matter with him?" murmured Ruth, and seized the paper herself.

She swiftly scrutinized the upper division of the first column of type. There were the usual requests for the return of absent friends, and several cryptic messages understood only by the advertiser and the person to whom the message was addressed.

The second "Personal" was different. It read as follows:

STRAYED,OR RUNAWAY FROM HIS GUARDIAN:— Boy, 15, slight figure, very light hair, may call himself Sorber, or Jakeway. His Guardian will pay FIFTY DOLLARS for information of his safety, or for his recovery. Address Twomley & Sorber's Herculean Circus and Menagerie, *en-route.*

Ruth read this through; but she read it idly. It made no more appeal to her just then than did half a dozen of the other advertisements—"personal," or otherwise.

So she carried the paper slowly upstairs, wondering all the time what Neale O'Neil could have seen in the column of advertising to so affect him. Perhaps had Agnes been at hand to discuss the matter, together the girls might have connected the advertisement of the tow-headed boy with Neale O'Neil.

But Agnes was out on an errand, and when she did return she was so full herself of something which she wished to tell Ruth that she quite drove thought of the white-haired boy, for the time being, out of the older girl's mind. As soon as she saw Ruth she began her tale.

"What do you think, Ruthie Kenway? I just met Eva Larry on the Parade, and that Trix Severn was with her. You know that Trix Severn?"

"Beatrice Severn? Yes," said Ruth, placidly. "A very well-dressed girl. Her parents must be well off."

"Her father is Terrence Severn, and he keeps a summer hotel at Pleasant Cove. But I don't like her. And I'm not going to like Eva if she makes a friend of that Trix," cried Agnes, stormily.

"Now, Agnes! don't be foolish," admonished Ruth.

"You wait till you hear what that nasty Trix said to me—about us all!"

"Why, she can't hurt us—much—no matter what she says," Ruth declared, still calmly.

"You can talk! I'm just going to tell Eva she needn't ask me to walk with her again when Trix is with her. I came along behind them across the Parade Ground and Eva called me. I didn't like Trix before, and I tried to get away.

"'I've got to hurry, Eva,' I said. 'Mrs. MacCall is waiting for this soap-powder.'"

"'I should think you Corner House girls could afford to hire somebody to run your errands, if you've got all the money they say you have,' says Trix Severn—just like that!"

"What did you reply, Aggie!" asked the older Kenway girl.

"'It doesn't matter how much, or how little, money we have,' I told her," said Agnes, "'there's no lazy-bones in our family, thank goodness!' For Eva told me that Trix's mother doesn't get up till noon and that their house is all at sixes and sevens."

"Oh! that sharp tongue of yours," said Ruth, admonishingly.

"I hope she took it," declared Agnes, savagely. "She said to me: 'Oh! people who haven't been used to leisure don't really know how to enjoy money, I suppose, when they *do* get it.'"

"'You needn't worry, Miss,' I said. 'We get all the fun there is going, and don't have to be idle, either. And whoever told *you* we weren't used to money before we came to Milton?'"

"Fie! Fie, Aggie! That was in the worst possible taste," cried Ruth.

"I don't care," exclaimed Agnes, stormily. "She's a nasty thing! And when I hurried on, I heard her laugh and say to Eva:

"''Put a beggar on horseback," you know. Miss Titus, the

dressmaker, says those Kenways never had two cents to bless themselves with before old crazy Peter Stower died and left them all that money.'"

"Well, dear, I wouldn't make a mountain out of a molehill," said Ruth, quietly. "If you don't like Beatrice Severn, you need not associate with her—not even if she is going to be in your grade at school. But I would not quarrel with my best friend about her. That's hardly worth while, is it?"

"I don't know whether I consider Eva Larry my best friend, or not," said Agnes, reflectively. "Myra Stetson is lots nicer in some ways."

That was Agnes' way. She was forever having a "crush" on some girl or other, getting suddenly over it, and seeking another affinity with bewildering fickleness. Eva Larry had been proclaimed her dearest friend for a longer term than most who had preceded her.

There was too much to do in completing the housecleaning task to spend either breath, or time, in discussing Beatrice Severn and her impudent tongue. A steady "rap, rap, rapping" from the back lawn told the story of Neale and the parlor rugs.

"There!" cried Ruth, suddenly, from the top of the step-ladder, where she was wiping the upper shelves in the dining-room china closet. "There's one rug in the sitting room I didn't take out last evening. Will you get it, Aggie, and give it to Neale?"

Willing Agnes started at once. She literally ran to the sitting-room and banged open the door.

All this time we have left Dot—and her sore tooth—behind

this very door! She had selected the wrong side of the door upon which to crouch, waiting for Fate—in the person of an unknowing sister—to pull the tooth.

The door opened inward, and against the slumbering little girl on the hassock. Instead of jerking the tooth out by pulling open the door, Agnes banged the door right against the unconscious Dot—and so hard that Dot and her hassock were flung some yards out upon the floor. Her forehead was bumped and a great welt raised upon it.

The smallest Kenway voiced her surprise and anguish in no uncertain terms. Everybody in the house came running to the rescue. Even Aunt Sarah came to the top of the stairs and wanted to know "if that young one was killed?"

"No-o-o!" sobbed Dot, answering for herself. "No—no-o-o, Aunt Sarah. *Not yet.*"

But Mrs. MacCall had brought the arnica bottle and the bruise was soon treated. While they were all comforting her, in staggered Neale with a number of rugs on his shoulder.

"Hello!" he demanded. "Who's murdered this time?"

"Me," proclaimed Dot, with confidence.

"Oh-ho! Are you making all that noise about losing a little old tooth? But you got it pulled, didn't you?"

Dot clapped a tentative finger into her mouth. When she drew it forth, it was with a pained and surprised expression. The place where the tooth should have been was empty.

"There it is," chuckled Neale, "hanging on the doorknob. Didn't I tell you that was the way to get your tooth pulled?"

"My!" gasped Dot. "It wasn't pulled out of me, you see. When Aggie ran in and knocked me over, *I was just putted away from the tooth*!"

They all burst out laughing at that, and Dot laughed with them. She recovered more quickly from the loss of her tooth than Agnes did from the loss of her temper!

CHAPTER VII

NEALE IN DISGUISE

The Parade Ground was in the center of Milton. Its lower end bordered Willow Street, and the old Corner House was right across from the termination of the Parade's principal shaded walk.

Ranged all around the Parade (which had in colonial days been called "the training ground" where the local militia-hands drilled) were the principal public buildings of the town, although the chief business places were situated down Main Street, below the Corner House.

The brick courthouse with its tall, square tower, occupied a prominent situation on the Parade. The several more important church edifices, too, faced the great, open common. Interspersed were the better residences of Milton. Some of these were far more modern than the old Stower homestead, but to the Kenway girls none seemed more homelike in appearance.

At the upper end of the Parade were grouped the schools of the town. There was a handsome new high school that Ruth was going to enter; the old one was now given over to the manual training departments. The grammar and primary

school was a large, sprawling building with plenty of ent-
rances and exits, and in this structure the other three Kenway
girls found their grades.

The quartette of Corner House girls were not the only young
folk anxious about entering the Milton schools for the forth-
coming year. There was Neale O'Neil. The Kenways knew
by the way he spoke, that his expected experiences at school
were uppermost in his thoughts all the time.

Ruth had talked the matter over with Mrs. MacCall, although
she had not seen Mr. Howbridge, and they had decided that
the boy was a very welcome addition to the Corner House
household, if he would stay.

But Neale O'Neil did not want charity—nor would he accept
anything that savored of it for long. Even while he was so
busy helping the girls clean house, he had kept his eyes and
ears open for a permanent lodging. And on Saturday
morning he surprised Ruth by announcing that he would
leave them after supper that night.

"Why, Neale! where are you going?" asked the oldest Corner
House girl. "I am sure there is room enough for you here."

"I know all about that," said Neale, grinning quickly at her.
"You folks are the best ever."

"Then, why—?"

"I've made a dicker with Mr. Con Murphy. You see, I won't
be far from you girls if you want me any time," he pursued.

"You are going to live with Mr. Murphy?"

"Yes. He's got a spare room—and it's very neat and clean.

There's a woman comes in and 'does' for him, as he calls it. He needs a chap like me to give him a hand now and then— taking care of the pig and his garden, you know."

"Not in the winter, Neale," said Ruth, gently. "I hope you are not leaving us for any foolish reason. You are perfectly welcome to stay. You ought to know that."

"That is fine of you, Ruth," he said, gratefully. "But you don't *need* me here. I can feel more independent over there at Murphy's. And I shall be quite all right there, I assure you."

The house was now all to rights—"spick and span," Mrs. MacCall said—and Saturday was given up to preparing for the coming school term. It was the last day of the long vacation.

Dot had no loose tooth to worry her and she was busy, with Tess, in preparing the dolls' winter nursery. All summer the little girls had played in the rustic house in the garden, but now that September had come, an out-of-door playroom would soon be too cold.

Although the great garret made a grand playroom for all hands on stormy days, Ruth thought it too far for Dot and Tess to go to the top of the house alone to play with their dolls. For her dolls were of as much importance to Dot as her own eating or sleeping. She lived in a little world of her own with the Alice-doll and all her other "children"; and she no more thought of neglecting them for a day than she and Tess neglected Billy Bumps or the cats.

There was no means of heating the garret, so a room in the wing with their bed chambers, and which was heated from the cellar furnace, was given up to "the kiddies'" nursery.

There were many treasures to be taken indoors, and Dot and Tess toiled out of the garden, and up the porch steps, and through the hall, and climbed the stairs to the new play-room—oh! so many times.

Mr. Stetson, the groceryman, came with an order just as Dot was toiling along with an armful to the porch.

"Hello! hello!" he exclaimed. "Don't you want some help with all that load, Miss Dorothy?" She was a special favorite of his, and he always stopped to talk with her.

"Ruthie says we got to move all by ourselves—Tess and me," said Dot, with a sigh. "I'm just as much obliged to you, but I guess you can't help."

She had sat down on the porch steps and Sandyface came, purring, to rub against her.

"You can go right away, Sandy!" said Dot, sternly. "I don't like you—much. You went and sat right down in the middle of my Alice-doll's old cradle, and on her best knit coverlet, and went to sleep—and you're moulting! I'll never get the hairs off of that quilt."

"Moulting, eh!" chuckled Mr. Stetson. "Don't you mean shedding?"

"We—ell, maybe," confessed Dot. "But the hens' feathers are coming out and they're moulting—I heard Ruth say so. So why not cats? Anyway, you can go away, Sandyface, and stop rubbing them off on *me*."

"What's become of that kitten of yours—Bungle, did you call it?" asked the groceryman.

"Why, don't you know?" asked Dot, in evident surprise.

"I haven't heard a word," confessed Mr. Stetson. "Did something happen to it?"

"Yes, sir."

"Was it poisoned?"

"Oh, no!"

"Drowned?"

"No, sir."

"Did somebody steal it?" queried Mr. Stetson.

"No, indeed!"

"Was it hurt in any way?"

"No, sir."

"Well, then," said the groceryman, "I can't guess. What *did* happen to Bungle?"

"Why," said Dot, "he growed into a cat!"

That amused Mr. Stetson immensely, and he went away, laughing. "It seems to me," Dot said, seriously, to Tess, "that it don't take so much to make grown-up people laugh. Is it funny for a kitten to grow into a cat?"

Neale disappeared for some time right after dinner. He had done all he could to help Uncle Rufus and Mrs. MacCall that forenoon, and had promised Ruth to come back for supper. "I wouldn't miss Mrs. MacCall's beans and fishcakes for a farm!" he declared, laughing.

But he did not laugh as much as he had when he first came to the old Corner House. Ruth, at least, noticed the change in him, and, "harking back," she began to realize that the change had begun just after Neale had been so startled by the advertisment he had read in the *Morning Post*.

The two older Kenway girls had errands to do at some of the Main Street stores that afternoon. It was Agnes who came across Neale O'Neil in the big pharmacy on the corner of Ralph Street. He was busily engaged with a clerk at the rear of the store.

"Hello, Neale!" cried Agnes. "What you buying?" Sometimes Agnes' curiosity went beyond her good manners.

"I'll take this kind," said Neale, hurriedly, touching a bottle at random, and then turned his back on the counter to greet Agnes. "An ounce of question-powders to make askits," he said to her, with a grave and serious air. "*You* don't need any, do you?"

"Funny!"

"But I don't *look* as funny as you do," chuckled Neale O'Neil. "That's the most preposterous looking hat I ever saw, Aggie. And those rabbit-ears on it!"

"Tow-head!" responded Agnes, with rather crude repartee.

Neale did not usually mind being tweaked about his flaxen hair—at least, not by the Corner House girls, but Agnes saw his expression change suddenly, and he turned back to the clerk and received his package without a word.

"Oh, you needn't get mad," she said, quickly.

"I'm not," responded Neale, briefly, but he paid for his purchase and hurried away without further remark. Agnes chanced to notice that the other bottles the clerk was returning to the shelves were all samples of dyes and "hair-restorers."

"Maybe he's buying something for Mr. Murphy. Mr. Murphy is awfully bald on top," thought Agnes, and that's all she *did* think about it until the next day.

The girls had invited Neale to go to their church, with them and he had promised to be there. But when they filed in just before the sermon they saw nothing of the white-haired boy standing about the porch with the other boys.

"There's somebody in our pew," whispered Tess to Ruth.

"Aunt Sarah?"

"No. Aunt Sarah is in her own seat across the aisle," said Agnes. "Why! it's a boy."

"It's Neale O'Neil," gasped Ruth. "But *what* has he done to his hair?"

A glossy brown head showed just above the tall back of the old-fashioned pew. The sun shining through the long windows on the side of the church shone upon Neale's thick thatch of hair with iridescent glory. Whenever he moved his head, the hue of the hair seemed to change—like a piece of changeable silk!

"That can't be him," said Agnes, with awe. "Where's all his lovely flaxen hair?"

"The foolish boy! He's dyed it," said Ruth, and then they reached the pew and could say no more.

Neale had taken the far corner of the pew, so the girls and Mrs. MacCall filed in without disturbing him. Agnes punched Neale with her elbow and scowled at him.

"What did you want to do that for?" she hissed.

"Do what for?" he responded, trying to look unconscious.

"You know. Fix your hair like that?"

"Because you called me 'tow-head,'" he whispered, grinning.

When Mrs. MacCall caught her first glimpse of him when they got up to sing, she started, stared, and almost expressed her opinion aloud.

"What under the canopy's the matter with that boy's head?" she whispered to Ruth when they were seated again.

And there was reason for asking! As the service proceeded and Neale's hair grew dryer, the sun shining upon his head revealed a wealth of iridescence that attracted more attention than the minister's sermon.

The glossy brown gave way before a greenish tinge that changed to purple at the roots. The dye would have been a success for an Easter egg, but as an application to the hair, it was not an unqualified delight—at least, not to the user.

The more youthful and thoughtless of the congregation— especially those behind the unconscious Neale—found amusement enough in the exhibition. The pastor discovered it harder than ever that morning to hold the attention of certain irreverent ones, and being a near-sighted man, he was at fault as to the reason for the bustle that increased as his sermon proceeded.

The Corner House girls—especially Ruth and Agnes—began to feel the matter acutely. Neale was quite unconscious of the result of the dye upon his hair. As the minutes passed and the rainbow effect became more and more visible, the disturbance became more pronounced.

Suddenly there sounded the important creaking of Deacon Abel's boots down the aisle. Agnes flashed a look over her shoulder. The stern old deacon was aiming straight for their pew!

CHAPTER VIII

INTRODUCTIONS

"Oh, goodness to gracious! Here comes old Mr. Abel—and he has fire in his eye, Ruth!" gasped Agnes.

"What—what's he going to do?" stammered Ruth, clinging to Agnes' hand under the hymn-book which they shared together.

"Something awful! Poor Neale!"

"His head looks a fright," declared Ruth.

"And everybody's laughing," groaned Agnes.

"Girls!" admonished Mrs. MacCall, "try to behave."

The creaking of the deacon's boots drew near. Old Mr. Abel kept a cut-price shoe shop and it was a joke among the young folk of Milton that all the shoes he sold were talking shoes, for when you walked in them they said very plainly:

"Cheap! cheap! cheap!"

Soon the minister noted the approach of Deacon Abel. As the

old man stopped by the Kenway pew, the minister lost the thread of his discourse, and stopped. A dread silence fell upon the church.

The deacon leaned forward in front of the little girls and Mrs. MacCall. His face was very red, and he shook an admonitory finger at the startled Neale O'Neil.

"Young man!" he said, sonorously. "Young man, you take off that wig and put it in your pocket—or leave this place of worship immediately."

It was an awful moment—especially awful for everybody in the Kenway pew. The girls' cheeks burned. Mrs. MacCall glared at the boy in utter stupefaction.

Deacon Abel was a very stern man indeed—much more so than the clergyman himself. All the young folk of the congregation stood in particular awe of him.

But poor Neale O'Neil, unconscious of any wrong intent, merely gazed at the old gentleman in surprise. "Wha— wha—*what*?" he gasped.

"Get out of here, young man!" exclaimed the deacon. "You have got the whole crowd by the ears. A most disgraceful exhibition. If I had the warming of your jacket I certainly would be glad."

"Oh!" exclaimed Ruth, horrified.

Agnes was really angry. She was an impulsive girl and she could not fail to espouse the cause of anybody whom she considered "put upon." She rose right up when Neale stumbled to his feet.

"Never you mind, Neale!" she whispered, shrilly. "He's a mean old thing! I'm coming, too."

It was a very wrong thing to say, but Agnes never stopped to think how a thing was going to sound when she was angry. The boy, his face aflame, got out through the next pew, which chanced to be empty, and Agnes followed right on behind him before Ruth could pull her back into her seat.

Nobody could have stopped her. She felt that Neale O'Neil was being ill-treated, and whatever else you could say about Aggie Kenway, you could not truthfully say that she was not loyal to her friends.

"Cheap! cheap! cheap!" squeaked the deacon's boots as he went back up one aisle while the boy and girl hurried up the other. It seemed to Neale as though the church was filled with eyes, staring at him.

His red face was a fine contrast for his rainbow-hued hair, but Agnes was as white as chalk.

The minister took up his discourse almost immediately, but it seemed to the culprits making their way to the door as though the silence had held the congregation for an hour! They were glad to get through the baize doors and let them swing together behind them.

Neale clapped his cap on his head, hiding a part of the ruin, but Deacon Abel came out and attacked him hotly:

"What do you mean by such disgraceful actions, boy?" he asked, with quivering voice. "I don't know who you are— you are a stranger to me; but I warn you never to come here and play such jokes again—"

"It isn't a joke, Mr. Abel!" cried Agnes.

"What do you call it, then? Isn't that one of them new-fangled wigs I read folks in the city wear to dances and other affairs? What's he got it on for?"

"It isn't a wig," Agnes said, while Neale clutched wildly at his hair.

"Don't tell me it's his own hair!" almost shouted the old gentleman.

"What's the matter with my hair?" demanded the puzzled boy.

"Doesn't he know? Do you mean to say he doesn't know what his head looks like?" cried the amazed deacon. "Come! come into this room, boy, and look at your hair."

There was the ushers' dressing-room at one end of the vestibule; he led Neale in by the arm. In the small mirror on the wall the boy got a fairly accurate picture of his hirsute adornment.

Without a word—after his first gasp of amazement—Neale turned and walked out of the room, and out of the church. It was a hot Sunday and the walks were bathed in sunshine. Neale involuntarily took the path across the Parade in the direction of the old Corner House.

At this hour—in the middle of sermon time—there was scarcely anybody in sight. Milton observed Sunday most particularly—especially in this better quarter of the town.

Neale had gone some way before he realized that Agnes was just beside him. He looked around at her and now his face was very pale.

"What did you come for?" he asked her, ungraciously enough.

"I'm so sorry, Neale," the girl whispered, drawing nearer to his elbow.

The boy stared for a moment, and then exclaimed: "Why, Aggie! you're a good little sport, all right."

Aggie blushed vividly, but she hastened to say: "Why did you do it, Neale?"

"I—I can't tell you," replied the boy, in some confusion. "Only I got to change the color of my hair."

"But, mercy! you needn't have changed it to so many colors all at once!" cried she.

"Huh! do you think—like that old man—that I did it a-purpose?"

"But you *did* dye it!"

"I tried to."

"That was the stuff you were buying yesterday in the drugstore?" she queried.

"Yes. And I put it on just before I started for church. He said it would make the hair a beautiful brown."

"*Who* said so?"

"That drugstore clerk," said Neale, despondently.

"He never sold you hair-dye at all!"

"Goodness knows what it was—"

"It's stained your collar—and it's run down your neck and dyed *that* green."

"Do you suppose I can ever get it off, Aggie?" groaned the boy.

"We'll try. Come on home and we'll get a lot of soapsuds in a tub in the woodshed—so we can splash it if we want to," said the suddenly practical Agnes.

They reached the woodshed without being observed by Uncle Rufus. Agnes brought the water and the soap and a hand-brush from the kitchen. Neale removed his collar and tie, and turned back the neck of his shirt. Agnes aproned her Sunday frock and went to work.

But, sad to relate, the more she scrubbed, and the more Neale suffered, the worse his hair looked!

"Goodness, Aggie!" he gasped at last. "My whole scalp is as sore as a boil. I don't believe I can stand your scrubbing it any more."

"I don't mean to hurt you, Neale," panted Agnes.

"I know it. But isn't the color coming out?"

"I—I guess it's *set*. Maybe I've done more harm than good. It's a sort of a sickly green all over. I never *did* see such a head of hair, Neale! And it was so pretty before."

"*Pretty!*" growled Neale O'Neil. "It was a nuisance.

Everybody who ever saw me remembered me as the 'white-haired boy.'"

"Well," sighed Agnes, "whoever sees that hair of yours *now* will remember you, and no mistake."

"And I have to go to school with it to-morrow," groaned Neale.

"It will grow out all right—in time," said the girl, trying to be comforting.

"It'll take more time than I want to spend with green hair," returned Neale. "I see what I'll have to do, Aggie."

"What's that?"

"Get a Riley cut. I don't know but I'd better be *shaved*."

"Oh, Neale! you'll look so funny," giggled Agnes, suddenly becoming hysterical.

"That's all right. You have a right to laugh," said Neale, as Agnes fell back upon a box to have her laugh out. "But I won't be any funnier looking with *no* hair than I would be with green hair—make up your mind to that."

Neale slipped over the back fence into Mr. Murphy's premises, before the rest of the Kenway family came home, and the girls did not see him again that day.

"How the folks stared at us!" Ruth said, shaking her head. "It would have been all right if you hadn't gotten up and gone out with him, Aggie."

"Oh, yes! let that horrid old Deacon Abel put him out of

church just as though he were a stray dog, and belonged to nobody!" cried Agnes.

"Well, he doesn't belong to us, does he?" asked Dot, wonderingly.

"We're the only folks he has, I guess, Dot," said Tess, as Agnes went off with her head in the air.

"He has Mr. Murphy—and the pig," said Dot, slowly. "But I like Neale. Only I wish he hadn't painted his hair so funny."

"I'd like to have boxed his ears—that I would!" said Mrs. MacCall, in vexation. "I thought gals was crazy enough nowadays; but to think of a *boy* dyeing his hair!"

Aunt Sarah shook her head and pursed her lips, as one who would say, "I knew that fellow would come to some bad end." But Uncle Rufus, having heard the story, chuckled unctuously to himself.

"Tell yo' what, chillen," he said to the girls, "it 'mind me ob de time w'en my Pechunia was a young, flighty gal. Dese young t'ings, dey ain't nebber satisfied wid de way de good Lawd make 'em.

"I nebber did diskiver w'y Pechunia was so brack, as I say afore. But 'tain't an affliction. She done t'ink it was. She done talk erbout face-bleach, an' powder, an' somet'ing she call 'rooch' wot white sassiety wimmens fixes up deir faces wid, an' says she ter me, 'Pap, I is gwine fin' some ob dese yere fixin's fur my complexion.'"

"'Yo' go 'long,' I says ter her. 'Yo's a *fast* brack, an' dat's all dere is to hit. Ef all de watah an' soap yo' done use ain't take no particle of dat soot off'n yo' yit, dere ain't nottin' eber *will* remove it.'"

"But yo' kyan't change a gal's natur. Pechunia done break her back ober de washtub ter earn de money to buy some o' dem make-up stuff, an' she goes down ter de drug sto' ter mak' her purchases. She 'low ter spen' much as six bits fer de trash.

"An' firs' t'ing she axed for was face powder—aw, my glo-ree! De clerk ask her: 'Wot shade does yo' want, Ma'am? An' Pechunia giggles an' replies right back:

"'Flesh color, Mister.'"

"An' wot you t'ink dat young scalawag ob a clerk gib her?" chuckled Uncle Rufus, rolling his eyes and shaking his head in delight. "W'y, he done gib her *powdered charcoal*! Dat finish Pechunia. She nebber tried to buy nottin' mo' for her complexion—naw, indeedy!"

The girls of the old Corner House learned that Neale was up early on Monday morning, having remained in hiding the remainder of Sunday. He sought out a neighbor who had a pair of sheep-shears, and Mr. Murphy cropped the boy's hair close to his scalp. The latter remained a pea-green color and being practically hairless, Neale looked worse than a Mexican dog!

He was not at all the same looking youth who had dawned on Agnes' vision the Monday morning previous, and had come to her rescue. She said herself she never would have known him.

"Oh, dear!" she said to Ruth. "He looks like a gnome out of a funny picture-book."

But Neale O'Neil pulled his cap down to his ears and

followed behind the Kenway girls to school. He was too proud and too sensitive to walk with them.

He knew that he was bound to be teased by the boys at school, when once they saw his head. Even the old cobbler had said to him:

"'Tis a foine lookin' noddle ye have now. Ye look like a tinder grane onion sproutin' out of the garden in the spring. Luk out as ye go over th' fince, me la-a-ad, for if that orma-dhoun of a goat sees ye, he'll ate ye alive!"

This was at the breakfast table, and Neale had flushed redly, being half angry with the old fellow.

"That's right, la-a-ad," went on Mr. Murphy. "Blushin' ain't gone out o' fashion where you kem from, I'm glad ter see. An' begorra! ye're more pathriotic than yer name implies, for I fear that's Scotch instead of Irish. I see now ye've put the grane above the red!"

So Neale went to school on this first day in no very happy frame of mind. He looked so much different with his hair cropped, from what he had at church on Sunday, that few of the young folks who had observed his disgrace there, recognized him—for which the boy was exceedingly glad.

He remained away from the Kenway girls, and in that way escaped recognition. He had to get acquainted with some of the fellows—especially those of the highest grammar grade. Being a new scholar, he had to meet the principal of the school, as well as Miss Shipman.

"Take your cap off, sir," said Mr. Marks, sternly. Unwillingly enough he did so. "For goodness' sake! what have you been doing to your head?" demanded the principal.

"Getting my hair clipped, sir," said Neale.

"But the color of your head?"

"That's why I had the hair clipped."

"What did you do to it?"

"It was an accident, sir," said Neale. "But I can study just as well."

"We will hope so," said the principal, his eyes twinkling. "But green is not a promising color."

Ruth had taken Dot to the teacher of the first grade, primary, and Dot was made welcome by several little girls whom she had met at Sunday school during the summer. Then Ruth hurried to report to the principal of the Milton High School, with whom she had already had an interview.

Tess found her grade herself. It was the largest room in the whole building and was presided over by Miss Andrews—a lady of most uncertain age and temper, and without a single twinkle in her grey-green eyes.

But with Tess were several girls she knew—Mable Creamer; Margaret and Holly Pease; Maria Maroni, whose father kept the vegetable and fruit stand in the cellar of one of the Stower houses on Meadow Street; Uncle Rufus' grand-daughter, Alfredia (with the big red ribbon bow); and a little Yiddish girl named Sadie Goronofsky, who lived with her step-mother and a lot of step-brothers and sisters in another of the tenements on Meadow Street which had been owned so many years by Uncle Peter Stower.

Agnes and Neale O 'Neil met in the same grade, but they did

not have a chance to speak, for the boys sat on one side of the room, and the girls on the other.

The second Kenway girl had her own troubles. During the weeks she lived at the old Corner House, she had been looking forward to entering school in the fall, so she had met all the girls possible who were to be in her grade.

Now she found that, school having opened, the girls fell right back into their old associations. There were the usual groups, or cliques. She would have to earn her place in the school, just as though she did not know a soul.

Beatrice, or "Trix" Severn, was not one of those whom Agnes was anxious to be friendly with; and here Trix was in the very seat beside her, while Eva Larry and Myra Stetson were across the room!

The prospect looked cloudy to Agnes, and she began the first school session with less confidence than any of her sisters.

CHAPTER IX

POPOCATEPETL IN MISCHIEF

Miss Georgiana Shipman was a plump lady in a tight bodice—short, dark, with a frankly double chin and eyes that almost always smiled. She did not possess a single beautiful feature; yet that smile of hers—friendly, appreciative of one's failings as well as one's successes—that smile cloaked a multitude of short-comings.

One found one's self loving Miss Georgiana—if one was a girl—almost at once; and the boldest and most unruly boy dropped his head and was ashamed to make Miss Georgiana trouble.

Sometimes boys with a long record of misdeeds behind them in other grades—misdeeds that blackened the pages of other teachers' deportment books—somehow managed to reach the door of Miss Georgiana's room without being dismissed from the school by the principal. Once having entered the favored portal, their characters seemed to change magically.

Mr. Marks knew that if he could bring the most abandoned scapegrace along in his studies so that he could spend a year with Miss Georgiana Shipman, in nine cases out of ten these hard-to-manage boys would be saved to the school. Sometimes they graduated at the very top of their classes.

Just as though Miss Georgiana were a fairy god-mother who struck her crutch upon the platform and cried: "Se sesame! *change!*" the young pirates often came through Miss Georgiana's hands and entered high school with the reputation of being very decent fellows after all.

Nor was Miss Georgiana a "softie"; far from it. Ask the boys themselves about it? Oh! they would merely hang their heads, and scrape a foot back and forth on the rug, and grunt: "Aw! Miss Shipman understands a fellow."

Her influence over the girls was even greater. She expected you to learn your lessons, and if you were lazy she spent infinite pains in urging you on. And if you did not work, Miss Georgiana felt aggrieved, and that made any nice girl feel dreadfully mean! Besides, you took up more of the teacher's time than you had any right to, and the other girls declared it was not fair, and talked pretty harshly about you.

If Miss Georgiana had to remain after school for any reason, more than half of her girls would be sure to hang around the school entrance until she came out, and then they all trailed home with her.

When you saw a bevy of girls from twelve to fourteen years of age, or thereabout, massed on one of the shady walks of the Parade soon after school closed for the day, or chattering along Whipple Street on which Miss Georgiana Shipman lived, you might be sure that the teacher of the sixth grade, grammar, was in the center of the group.

Miss Georgiana lived with her mother—a little old lady in Quaker dress—in a small cottage back from the street-line.

There were three big oaks in the front yard, and no grass ever could be coaxed to grow under them, for the girls kept it worn down to the roots.

There were seats at the roots of the three huge trees in the open season, and it was an odd afternoon indeed that did not find a number of girls here. To be invited to stay to tea at Miss Georgiana's was the height of every girl's ambition who belonged in Number Six.

Nor did the girls when graduated, easily forget Miss Georgiana. She had their confidence and some of them came to her with troubles and perplexities that they could have exposed to nobody else.

Of course, girls who had "understanding" mothers, did not need this special inspiration and help, but it was noticeable that girls who had no mothers at all, found in the little, plump, rather dowdy "old maid school teacher" one of those choice souls that God has put on earth to fulfil the duties of parents taken away.

Miss Georgiana Shipman had been teaching for twenty years, but she had never grown old. And her influence was— to use a trite description—like a stone flung into a still pool of water; the ever widening circles set moving by it lapped the very outer shores of Milton life.

Of course Agnes Kenway was bound to fall in love with this teacher; and Miss Georgiana soon knew her for just the "stormy petrel" that she was. Agnes gravitated to scrapes as naturally as she breathed, but she got out of them, too, as a usual thing without suffering any serious harm.

Trix Severn annoyed her. Trix had it in her power to bother the next to the oldest Corner House girl, sitting as she did at the nearest desk. The custom was, in verbal recitation, for the pupil to rise in her (or his) seat and recite. When it came Agnes' time to recite, Trix would whisper something entirely irrelevant to the matter before the class.

This sibilant monologue was so nicely attuned by Trix that Miss Georgiana (nor many of the girls besides Agnes herself) did not hear it. But it got on Agnes' nerves and one afternoon, before the first week of school was over, she turned suddenly on the demure Trix in the middle of her recitation and exclaimed, hysterically:

"If you don't stop whispering that way, Trix Severn, I'll just go mad!"

"Agnes!" ejaculated Miss Shipman. "What does this mean?"

"I don't care!" cried Agnes, stormily. "She interrupts me—"

"Didn't either!" declared Trix, thereby disproving her own statement in that particular case, at least. "I didn't speak to her."

"You did!" insisted Agnes.

"Agnes! sit down," said Miss Shipman, and sternly enough, for the whole room was disturbed. "What *were* you doing, Beatrice?"

"Just studying, Miss Shipman," declared Trix, with perfect innocence.

"This is not the time for study, but for recitation. You need not recite, and I will see both of you after school. Go on from where Agnes left off, Lluella."

"I'll fix you for this!" hissed Trix to Agnes. Agnes felt too badly to reply and the jealous girl added: "You Corner House girls think you are going to run things in this school, I suppose; but you'll see, Miss! You're nothing but upstarts."

Agnes did not feel like repeating this when Miss Georgiana made her investigation of the incident after school. She was no "tell-tale."

Therefore she repeated only her former accusation that Trix's whispering had confused her in her recitation.

"I never whispered to her!" snapped Trix, tossing her head. "I'm not so fond of her as all that, I hope."

"Why, I expect all my girls to be fond of each other," said Miss Georgiana, smiling, "too, too fond to hurt each other's feelings, or even to annoy each other."

"She just put it all on," sniffed Trix.

"Agnes is nervous," said the teacher, quietly, "but she must learn to control her nerves and not to fly into a passion and be unladylike. Beatrice, you must not whisper and annoy your neighbors. I hope you two girls will never take part in such an incident again while you are with me."

Agnes said, "I'm sorry, Miss Shipman," but when the teacher's back was turned, Trix screwed her face into a horrid mask and ran out her tongue at Agnes. Her spitefulness fairly boiled over.

This was the first day Agnes had been late getting home, so she missed the first part of an incident of some moment. Popocatepetl got herself on this day into serious mischief.

Popocatepetl (she was called "Petal" for short) was one of Sandyface's four kittens that had been brought with the old cat from Mr. Stetson's grocery to the old Corner House, soon after the Kenway girls came to live there. Petal was Ruth's particular pet—or, had been, when she was a kitten. Agnes' choice was the black one with the white nose, called Spotty; Tess's was Almira, while Dot's—as we already know—was called Bungle, and which, to Dot's disgust, had already "grown up."

All four of the kittens were good sized cats now, but they were not yet of mature age and now and then the girls were fairly convulsed with laughter because of the antics of Sandyface's quartette of children.

There was to be a pair of ducks for Sunday's dinner and Uncle Rufus had carefully plucked them into a box in a corner of the kitchen, so that the down would not be scattered. Mrs. MacCall was old-fashioned enough to save all duck and geese down for pillows.

When the oldest and the two youngest Kenway girls trooped into the kitchen, Popocatepetl was chasing a stray feather about the floor and in diving behind the big range for it, she knocked down the shovel, tongs and poker, which were standing against the bricked-up fireplace.

The clatter scared Petal immensely, and with tail as big as three ordinary tails and fur standing erect upon her back, she shot across the kitchen and into the big pantry.

Uncle Rufus had just taken the box of feathers into this room and set it down on the floor, supposedly out of the way. Mrs. MacCall was measuring molasses at the table, for a hot gingerbread-cake was going to grace the supper-table.

"Scat, you cat, you!" exclaimed Uncle Rufus. "Dar's too many of you cats erbout disher house, an' dat's a fac'. Dar's more cats dan dar is mices to ketch—ya-as'm!"

"Oh, Uncle Rufus! you don't mean that, do you?" asked Tess, the literal. "Aren't there as many as five mice left? You know you said yourself there were hundreds before Sandyface and her children came."

"Glo-*ree*! I done s'peck dey got down to purty few numbers," agreed Uncle Rufus. "Hi! wot dat cat do now?"

"Scat!" cried Mrs. MacCall. She had left the table for a moment, and Popocatepetl was upon it.

"Petal!" shrieked Ruth, and darted for the pantry to seize her pet.

All three scolding her, and making for her, made Popocatepetl quite hysterical. She arched her back, spit angrily, and then dove from the table. In her flight she overturned the china cup of molasses which fell to the floor and broke. The sticky liquid was scattered far and wide.

"That kitten!" Mrs. MacCall shrieked.

"Wait! wait!" begged Ruth, trying to grab up Petal.

But the cat dodged her and went right through the molasses on the floor. All her four paws were covered. Wherever she stepped she left an imprint. And when the excited Ruth grabbed for her again, she capped her ridiculous performance by leaping right into the box of feathers!

Finding herself hopelessly "stuck-up" now, Popocatepetl went completely crazy!

She leaped from the box, scattering a trail of sticky feathers behind her. She made a single lap around the kitchen trying for an outlet, faster than any kitten had ever traveled before in that room.

"Stop her!" shrieked Ruth.

"My clean kitchen!" wailed Mrs. MacCall.

"Looker dem fedders! looker dem fedders!" gasped Uncle Rufus. "She done got dem all stuck on her fo' sho'!"

"Oh, oh!" squealed Tess and Dot, in chorus, and clinging together as Petal dashed past them.

Just at this moment Agnes opened the door and saw what appeared to be an animated feather-boa dashing about the kitchen, with the bulk of the family in pursuit.

"What for goodness' sake is the matter?" gasped Agnes.

Popocatepetl saw the open door and she went through it as though she had been shot out of a gun, leaving a trail of feathers in her wake and splotches of molasses all over the kitchen floor.

CHAPTER X

THE ICE STORM

The four girls followed Popocatepetl out of the house in a hurry. Their shrill voices aroused Neale O'Neil where he was spading up a piece of Mr. Con Murphy's garden for a planting of winter spinach. He came over the fence in a hurry and ran up the long yard.

"What's the matter? What's the matter?" he shouted.

The chorus of explanation was so confused that Neale might never have learned the difficulty to this very moment, had he not looked up into the bare branches of the Keifer pear tree and seen an object clinging close to a top limb.

"For pity's sake!" he gasped. "What is that?"

"It's Petal," shrilled Dot. "An' she's felled into the merlasses and got herself all feathers."

At that her sisters burst out laughing. It was too bad the little cat was so frightened, but it *was* too comical for anything!

"You don't call that a cat?" demanded Neale, when he could control his own risibilities.

"Of course it's a cat," said Tess, rather warmly. "You know Ruthie's Popocatepetl, Neale—you know you do."

"But a thing with feathers, roosting in a tree, must be some kind of a fowl—yes?" asked Neale, with gravity.

"It's a cat-bird," announced Agnes.

The younger girls could not see any fun in the situation. Poor Petal, clinging to the high branch of the tree, and faintly mewing, touched their hearts, so Neale went up like a professional acrobat and after some difficulty brought the frightened cat down.

"She'll have to be plucked just like a chicken," declared Ruth. "Did you *ever* see such a mess in all your life?"

Neale held the cat so she could not scratch, and Agnes and Ruth "plucked" her and wiped off the molasses as best they could. But it was several days before Popocatepetl was herself again.

By this time, too, Neale O'Neil's green halo was beginning to wear off. As Mr. Con Murphy said, he looked less like "a blushin' grane onion" than he had immediately after the concoction the drugstore clerk had sold him took effect.

"And 'tis hopin' 'twill be a lesson ye'll allus remimber," pursued the old cobbler. "Niver thrust too much to whativer comes in a bottle! Remimber 'tis not the label ye air to use. The only r'ally honest label that kems out of a drug-sthore is thim that has the skull and crossbones on 'em. You kin be sure of them; they're pizen an' no mistake!"

Neale had to listen to a good deal that was harder to bear than any of Mr. Murphy's quaint philosophy. But he restrained himself and did not fight any boy going to school.

In the first place, Neale O'Neil was going to school for just one purpose. He wished to learn. To boys and girls who had always had the advantages of school, this desire seemed strange enough. They could not understand Neale.

And because of his earnestness about study, and because he refused to tell anything about himself, they counted Neale odd. The Corner House girls were the only real friends the boy had in Milton among the young folk. But some older people began to count Neale as a boy of promise.

Green as his head was dyed, it was a perfectly good head when it came to study, as he had assured Mr. Marks. The principal watched the youngster and formed a better opinion of him than he had at first borne. Miss Shipman found him a perfectly satisfactory scholar.

The people he worked for at odd jobs, after and before school, learned that he was faithful and smart. Mr. Con Murphy had a good word for the boy to everybody who came into his shop.

Yet, withal, he could not make close friends. One must give confidence for confidence if one wishes to make warm friendships. And Neale was as secretive as he could be.

Neale kept close to the neighborhood of the cobbler's and the old Corner House. Agnes told Ruth that she believed Neale never turned a corner without first peeking around it! He was always on the *qui vive*—expecting to meet somebody of whom he was afraid. And every morning he ran over to the Corner House early and looked at the first column on the front page of the *Morning Post*, as it lay on the big veranda.

The four Corner House girls all achieved some distinction in their school grades within the first few weeks of the fall term. Ruth made friends as she always did wherever she went. Other girls did not get a sudden "crush" on Ruth Kenway, and then as quickly forget her. Friendship for her was based upon respect and admiration for her sense and fine qualities of character.

Agnes fought her way as usual to the semi-leadership of her class, Trix Severn to the contrary notwithstanding. She was not quite as good friends with Eva Larry as she had been, and had soon cooled a trifle toward Myra Stetson, but there were dozens of other girls to pick and choose from, and in rotation Agnes became interested in most of those in her grade.

Tess was the one who came home with the most adventures to tell. There always seemed to be "something doing" in Miss Andrews' room.

"We're all going to save our money toward a Christmas tree for our room," Tess announced, long before cold weather had set in "for keeps." "Miss Andrews says we can have one, but those that aren't good can have nothing to do with it. I'm afraid," added Tess, seriously, "that not many of the boys in our grade will have anything to do with that tree."

"Is Miss Andrews so dreadfully strict?" asked Dot, round-eyed.

"Yes, she is—awful!"

"I hope she'll get married, then, and leave school before I get into her grade."

"But maybe she won't ever marry," Tess declared.

"Don't all ladies marry—some time?" queried Dot, in surprise.

"Aunt Sarah never did, for one."

"Oh—well—Don't you suppose there's enough men to go 'round, Tess?" cried Dot, in some alarm. "Wouldn't it be dreadful to grow up like Aunt Sarah—or your Miss Andrews?"

Tess tossed her head. "I am going to be a suffragette," she announced. "They don't have to have husbands. Anyway, if they have them," qualified Tess, "they don't never bother about them much!"

Tess' mind, however, was full of that proposed Christmas tree. Maria Maroni was going to bring an orange for each pupil—girls and boys alike—to be hung on the tree. Her father had promised her that.

Alfredia Blossom, Jackson Montgomery Simms Blossom, and Burne-Jones Whistler Blossom had stored bushels of hickory nuts and butternuts in the cockloft of their mother's cabin, and they had promised to help fill the stockings that the girls' sewing class was to make.

Every girl of Tess' acquaintance was going to do something "lovely," and she wanted to know what *she* could do?

"Why, Sadie Goronofsky says maybe she'll *buy* something to hang on the tree. She is going to have a lot of money saved by Christmas time," declared Tess.

"Why, Tess," said Agnes, "isn't Sadie Goronofsky Mrs. Goronofsky's little girl that lives in one of our tenements on Meadow Street?"

"No. She's *Mister* Goronofsky's little girl. The lady Mr. Goronofsky married is only Sadie's step-mother. She told me so."

"But they are very poor people," Ruth said. "I know, for they can scarcely pay their rent some months. Mr. Howbridge told me so."

"There are a lot of little children in the family," said Agnes.

"And Sadie is the oldest," Tess said. "You see, she told me how it was. She has to go home nights and wash and dry the dishes, and sweep, and take care of the baby—and lots of things. She never has any time to play.

"But on Friday night—that's just like our Saturday night, you know," explained Tess, "for they celebrate Saturday as Sunday—they're Jewish people. Well, on Friday night, Sadie tells me, her step-mother puts a quarter for her in a big red bank in their kitchen."

"Puts a quarter each week in Sarah's bank?" said Ruth. "Why, that's fine!"

"Yes. It's because Sadie washes the dishes and takes care of the baby so nice. And before Christmas the bank is going to be opened. Then Sadie is going to get something nice for all her little step-brothers and sisters, and something nice for our tree, too."

"She'll have a lot of money," said Agnes. "Must be they're not so poor as they make out, Ruth."

"Mr. Goronofsky has a little tailor business, and that's all," Ruth said, gravely. "I—I sha'n't tell Mr. Howbridge about Sadie and her bank."

Thanksgiving came and went—and it was a real Thanksgiving for the Corner House girls. They had never had such a fine time on that national festival before, although they were all alone—just the regular family—at the table.

Neale was to have helped eat the plump hen turkey that Mrs. MacCall roasted, but the very night before Thanksgiving he came to Ruth and begged off.

"I got to talking with Mr. Murphy this afternoon," said Neale, rather shamefacedly, "and he said he hadn't eaten a Thanksgiving dinner since his wife and child drowned in the Johnstown flood—and that was years and years ago, you know.

"So I asked him if he'd have a good dinner if I stayed and ate it with him, and the old fellow said he would," Neale continued. "And Mrs. Judy Roach—the widow woman who does the extra cleaning for him—will come to cook the dinner.

"He's gone out to buy the turkey—the biggest gobbler he can get, he told me—for Mrs. Judy has a raft of young ones, 'all av thim wid appetites like a famine in ould Ireland,' he told me."

"Oh, Neale!" cried Ruth, with tears in her eyes.

"He's a fine old man," declared Neale, "when you get under the skin. Mrs. Judy Roach and her brood will get a square meal for once in their lives—believe me."

So Neale stayed at the cobbler's and helped do the honors of that Thanksgiving dinner. He reported to the Corner House girls later how it "went off."

"'For phat we are about to resave,' as Father Dooley says—

Aloysius, ye spalpane! ye have an eye open, squintin' at the tur-r-rkey!—'lit us be trooly thankful,'" observed Mr. Con Murphy, standing up to carve the huge, brown bird. "Kape your elbows off the table, Aloysius Roach—ye air too old ter hev such bad manners. What par-r-rt of the bir-r-d will ye have, Aloysius?"

"A drumstick," announced Aloysius.

"A drumstick it is—polish that now, ye spalpane, and polish it well. And Alice, me dear, phat will *youse* hev?" pursued Mr. Murphy.

"I'll take a leg, too, Mr. Murphy," said the oldest Roach girl.

"Quite right. Iv'ry par-r-rt stringthens a par-r-rt—an' 'tis a spindle-shanks I notice ye air, Alice. And you, Patrick Sarsfield?" to the next boy.

"Leg," said Patrick Sarsfield, succinctly.

Mr. Murphy dropped the carver and fork, and made a splotch of gravy on the table.

"*What?*" he shouted. "Hev ye not hear-r-rd two legs already bespoke, Patrick Sarsfield, an' ye come back at me for another? Phat for kind of a baste do ye think this is? I'm not carvin' a cinterpede, I'd hev ye know!"

At last the swarm of hungry Roaches was satisfied, and, according to Neale's report, the dinner went off very well indeed, save that his mother feared she would have to grease and roll Patrick Sarsfield before the fire to keep him from bursting, he ate so much!

It was shortly after Thanksgiving that Milton suffered from

its famous ice-storm. The trees and foliage in general suffered greatly, and the *Post* said there would probably be little fruit the next year. For the young folk of the town it brought great sport.

The Corner House girls awoke on that Friday morning to see everything out-of-doors a glare of ice. The shade trees on the Parade were borne down by the weight of the ice that covered even the tiniest twig on every tree. Each blade of grass was stiff with an armor of ice. And a scum of it lay upon all the ground.

The big girls put on their skates and dragged Tess and Dot to school. Almost all the older scholars who attended school that day went on steel. At recess and after the session the Parade was the scene of races and impromptu games of hockey.

The girls of the sixth grade, grammar, held races of their own. Trix Severn was noted for her skating, and heretofore had been champion of all the girls of her own age, or younger. She was fourteen—nearly two years older than Agnes Kenway.

But Agnes was a vigorous and graceful skater. She skated with Neale O'Neil (who at once proved himself as good as any boy on the ice) and *that* offended Trix, for she had wished to skate with Neale herself.

Since the green tinge had faded out of Neale's hair, and it had grown to a respectable length, the girls had all cast approving glances at him. Oddly enough, his hair had grown out a darker shade than before. It could not be the effect of the dye, but he certainly was no longer "the white-haired boy."

Well! Trix was real cross because Agnes Kenway skated

with Neale. Then, when the sixth grade, grammar, girls got up the impromptu races, Trix found that Agnes was one of her closest competitors.

While the boys played hockey at the upper end of the Parade, the girls raced 'way to Willow Street and back again. Best two out of three trials it was, and the first trial was won by Agnes—and she did it easily!

"Why! you've beaten Trix," Eva Larry cried to Agnes. "However did you do it? She always beats us skating."

"Oh, I broke a strap," announced Trix, quickly. "Come on! we'll try it again, and I'll show you."

"I believe Agnes can beat you every time, Trix," laughed Eva, lightly.

Trix flew into a passion at this. And of course, all her venom was aimed at Agnes.

"I'll show that upstart Corner House girl that she sha'n't ride over *me*," she declared, angrily, as the contestants gathered for the second trial of speed.

CHAPTER XI

THE SKATING RACE

There were nearly thirty girls who lined up for the second heat. Many who had tried the first time dropped out, having been distanced so greatly by the leaders.

"But that is no way to do!" laughed Agnes, ignoring Trix Severn and her gibes. "It is anybody's race yet. One never knows what may happen in a free-for-all like this. Trix, or Eva, or I, may turn an ankle—"

"Or break another strap," broke in Eva, laughing openly at Trix.

"Just you wait!" muttered Trix Severn, in a temper.

Now, giving way to one's temper never helps in a contest of strength or skill. Agnes herself was trying to prove that axiom; but Trix had never tried to restrain herself.

Ere this Miss Shipman had changed Agnes' seat in the class-room, seeing plainly that Trix continued her annoying actions; Agnes had striven to be patient because she loved Miss Shipman and did not want to make trouble in her grade.

Agnes took her place now as far from Trix as she could get. Ruth, and another of the older girls were at the line, and one of the high school boys who owned a stop-watch timed the race.

"Ready!" he shouted. "Set!"

The race was from a dead start. The girls bent forward, their left feet upon the mark.

"Go!" shouted the starter.

The smoothest stretch of ice was right down the center of the Parade. It was still so cold that none of the trees had begun to drip. Some employees of the town Highway Department were trying to knock the ice off the trees, so as to save the overweighted branches.

But thus far these workmen had kept away from the impromptu race-course. Down the middle of the park the girls glided toward the clump of spruce trees, around which they must skate before returning.

Trix, Eva, Myra, Pearl Harrod and Lucy Poole all shot ahead at the start. Agnes "got off on the wrong foot," as the saying is, and found herself outdistanced at first.

But she was soon all right. She had a splendid stroke for a girl, and she possessed pluck and endurance.

She crept steadily up on the leading contestants, passing Eva, Myra, and Lucy before half the length of the Parade Ground was behind them.

Trix was in the lead and Pearl Harrod was fighting her for first place.

Agnes kept to one side and just before the trio reached the spruce clump at Willow Street, she shot in, rounded the clump alone, and started up the course like the wind upon the return trip!

Trix fairly screamed after her, she was so vexed. Trix, too, had endurance. She left Pearl behind and skated hard after Agnes Kenway.

She never would have caught her, however, had it not been for an odd accident that happened to the Corner House girl.

As Agnes shot up the course, one of the workmen came with a long pole with a hook on the end of it, and began to shake the bent branches of a tree near the skating course. Off rattled a lot of ice, falling to the hard surface below and breaking into thousands of small bits.

Agnes was in the midst of this rubbish before she knew it. One skate-runner got entangled in some pieces and down she went—first to her knees and then full length upon her face!

Some of the other girls shrieked with laughter. But it might have been a serious accident, Agnes was skating so fast.

Trix saved her breath to taunt her rival later, and, skating around the bits of ice, won the heat before Agnes, much shaken and bruised, had climbed to her feet.

"Oh, Aggie! you're not really hurt, are you?" cried Ruth, hurrying to her sister.

"My goodness! I don't know," gasped Agnes. "I saw stars."

"You have a bump on your forehead," said one girl.

"I feel as though I had them all over me," groaned Agnes.

"I know that will turn black and blue," said Lucy, pointing to the lump on Agnes' forehead.

"And yellow and green, too," admitted Agnes. Then she giggled and added in a whisper to Ruth: "It will be as brilliant as Neale's hair was when he dyed it!"

"Well, you showed us what you could do in the first heat, Aggie," said Pearl, cheerfully. "I believe that you can easily beat Trix."

"Oh, yes!" snarled the latter girl, who over-heard this. "A poor excuse for not racing is better than none."

"Well! I declare, Trix, if *you'd* fallen down," began Eva; but Agnes interrupted:

"I haven't said I wasn't going to skate the third heat."

"Oh! you can't, Aggie," Ruth said.

"I'd skate it if I'd broken both legs and all my promises!" declared Agnes, sharply. "That girl isn't going to put it all over me without a fight!"

"Great!" cried Eva. "Show her."

"I admire your pluck, but not your language, Aggie," said her older sister. "And if you *can* show her—"

Agnes did show them all. She had been badly shaken up by her fall, and her head began to throb painfully, but the color had come back into her cheeks and she took her place in the line of contestants again with a bigger determination than ever to win.

She got off on the right foot this time! Only eighteen girls started and all of them were grimly determined to do their best.

The boys had left off their hockey games and crowded along the starting line and the upper end of the track, to watch the girls race. People had come out from their houses to get a closer view of the excitement, and some of the teachers—including Mr. Marks and the physical instructors—were in the crowd. The boys began to root for their favorites, and Agnes heard Neale leading the cheers for her.

Trix Severn was not much of a favorite with the boys; she wasn't "a good sport." But the second Kenway girl had showed herself to be good fun right from the start.

"Got it, Agnes! Hurrah for the Corner House girl!" shrieked one youngster who belonged in the sixth grade, grammar.

"Eva Larry for mine," declared another. "She's some little skater, and don't you forget it."

Some of the boys started down the track after the flying contestants, but Ruth darted after them and begged them to keep out of the way so as not to confuse the racers when they should come back up the Parade Ground.

Meanwhile Agnes was taking no chances of being left behind this time. She had gotten off right and was in the lead within the first few yards. Putting forth all her strength at first, she easily distanced most of the eighteen. It was, after all, a short race, and she knew that she must win it "under the whip," if at all.

Her fall would soon stiffen and lame her; Agnes knew that very well. Ordinarily she would have given in to the pain she felt and owned that she had been hurt. But Trix's taunts were hard to bear—harder than the pain in her knee and in her head.

Once she glanced over her shoulder and saw Trix right behind—the nearest girl to her in the race. The glance inspired her to put on more steam. She managed to lead the crowd to the foot of the Parade.

She turned the clump of spruce trees on the "long roll" and found a dozen girls right at her heels as she faced up the Parade again. Trix was in the midst of them.

There was some confusion, but Agnes kept out of it. She had her wits very much about her, too; and she saw that Trix cut the spruce clump altogether—turning just before reaching the place, and so saving many yards.

In the excitement none of the other racers, save Agnes, noticed this trick. "Cheat!" thought Agnes. But the very fact that her enemy was dishonest made Agnes the more determined to beat her.

Agnes' breath was growing short, however; *how* her head throbbed! And her right knee felt as though the skin was all abrased and the cap fairly cracked. Of course, she knew this last could not be true, or she would not be skating at all; but she was in more pain than she had ever suffered in her life before without "giving in" to it.

She gritted her teeth and held grimly to her course. Trix suddenly pulled up even with her. Agnes knew the girl never would have done so had she not cheated at the bottom of the course.

"I'll win without playing baby, or I won't win at all!" the Corner House girl promised herself. "If she can win after cheating, let her!"

And it looked at the moment as though Trix had the better chance. She drew ahead and was evidently putting forth all her strength to keep the lead.

Right ahead was the spot where the broken ice covered the course. Agnes bore well away from it; Trix swept out, too, and almost collided with her antagonist.

"Look where you're going! Don't you dare foul me!" screamed the Severn girl at Agnes.

That flash of rage cost Trix something. Agnes made no reply—not even when Trix flung back another taunt, believing that the race was already won.

But it was not. "I will! *I will!*" thought Agnes, and she stooped lower and shot up the course passing Trix not three yards from the line, and winning by only an arm's length.

"I beat her! I beat her!" cried Trix, blinded with tears, and almost falling to the ice. "Don't you dare say I didn't."

"It doesn't take much courage to say that, Beatrice," said Miss Shipman, right at her elbow. "We all saw the race. It was fairly won by Agnes."

"It wasn't either! She's a cheat!" gasped the enraged girl, without realizing that she was speaking to her teacher instead of to another girl.

This was almost too much for Agnes' self-possession. She was in pain and almost hysterical herself. She darted forward and demanded:

"Where did *I* cheat, Miss? You can't say *I* didn't skate around the spruce clump down there."

"That's right, Aggie," said the high school girl who had been on watch with Ruth. "I saw Trix cut that clump, and if she'd gotten in first, she'd have lost on that foul."

"That's a story!" exclaimed Trix; but she turned pale.

"Say no more about it, girls. The race is won by Agnes—and won honestly," Miss Georgiana said.

But Trix Severn considered she had been very ill-used by Agnes. She buried *that* bone and carefully marked the spot where it lay.

CHAPTER XII

THE CHRISTMAS PARTY

"What do you think Sammy Pinkney said in joggerfry class to-day?" observed Tess, one evening at the supper table.

"'Geography,' dear. Don't try to shorten your words so," begged Ruth.

"I—I forgot," admitted Tess. "'Ge-og-er-fry!' Is that right?"

"Shucks!" exclaimed Agnes. "Let's have the joke. I bet Sammy Pinkney is always up to something."

"He likes Tess, Sammy does," piped up Dot, "for he gave her Billy Bumps."

Tess grew fiery red. "I don't want boys liking me!" she declared. "Only Neale."

"And especially not Sam Pinkney, eh?" said Agnes. "But what happened? You have us all worked up, Tess."

"Why, Miss Andrews was telling us that the 'stan' at the end of any word meant 'the place of'—like Afghanistan, the place the Afghans live—"

"That's what Mrs. Adams is knitting," interposed Dot, placidly.

"*What?*" demanded Agnes. "Why, the Afghans are a people —in Asia—right near India."

"She's knitting one; she told me so," declared Dot, holding her ground obstinately. "She knits it out of worsted."

"That's right," laughed Ruth. "It's a crocheted 'throw' for a couch. You are right, Dot; and so are you, too, Aggie."

"Are we ever going to get to Sammy Pinkney?" groaned Agnes.

"Well!" said Tess, indignantly, "I'll tell you, if you'll give me a chance."

"Sail right in, sister," chuckled Agnes.

"So Miss Andrews said 'stan' meant 'the place of,'" rushed on Tess, "like Afghanistan, and Hindoostan, 'the place of the Hindoos,' and she says:

"'Can any of you give another example of the use of "stan" for the end of a word?' and Sammy says:

"'I can, Miss Andrews. Umbrellastan—the place of the umbrellars,' and now Sammy," concluded Tess, "can't have any stocking on our Christmas tree."

"I guess Sammy was trying to be smart," said Dot, gravely.

"He's a smart boy, all right," Agnes chuckled. "I heard him last Sunday in Sunday school class. He's in Miss Pepperill's class right behind ours. Miss Pepperill asked Eddie Collins:

"'What happened to Babylon?'"

"'It fell,' replied Ed."

"'And what happened to Sodom and Gomorrah?' she asked Robbie Foote, and Robbie said:"

"'They were destroyed, Miss Pepperill.'"

"Then she came to Sammy. 'What of Tyre, Sammy?' she asked."

"'Punctured,' said Sammy, and got the whole class to laughing."

"Oh, now, Aggie!" queried Ruth, doubtfully, "isn't that a joke?"

"No more than Tess's story is a joke," giggled the plump girl.

"But it's no joke for Sammy to lose his part in the Christmas entertainment," said Tess, seriously. "I'm going to buy him a pair of wristlets, his wrists are so chapped."

"You keep on planning to buy presents for all the boys that are shut out of participating in the Christmas tree," laughed Ruth, "and you'll use up all your spending money, Tess."

Tess was reflective. "Boys are always getting into trouble, aren't they?" she observed. "It's lucky we haven't any in this family."

"I think so myself, Tess," agreed Ruth.

"Well! Nice boys like Neale," spoke up the loyal Dot, "wouldn't hurt any family."

"But there aren't many nice ones like Neale," said Tess, with conviction. "'Most always they seem to be getting into trouble and being punished. The teachers don't like them much."

"Oh, *our* teacher does," said Dot, eagerly. "There's Jacob Bloomer. You know—his father is the German baker on Meadow Street. Our teacher used to like him a lot."

"And what's the matter with Jakey now?" asked Agnes. "Is he in her bad books?"

"I don't know would you call it 'bad books,'" Dot said. "But he doesn't bring the teacher a pretzel any more."

"A pretzel!" exclaimed Ruth.

"What a ridiculous thing to bring," said Agnes.

"She liked them," Dot said, nodding. "But she doesn't eat them any more."

"Why not?" asked Ruth.

"We—ell, Jacob doesn't bring them."

"Do tell us why not!"

"Why," said Dot, earnestly, "you see teacher told Jacob one day that she liked them, but she wished his father didn't make them so salty. So after that Jacob always brought teacher a pretzel without any salt on it.

"'It's very kind,' teacher told Jacob, 'of your father to make me a pretzel 'specially every day,' she told him, 'without the salt.' And Jacob told her his father didn't do any such thing;

he licked the salt off before he gave teacher the pretzel—an' she hasn't never eaten any since, and Jacob's stopped bringing them," concluded Dot.

"Well! what do you think of that?" gasped Agnes. "I should think your teacher *would* lose her taste for pretzels."

"But I don't suppose Jacob understands," said Ruth, smiling.

"Oh, Ruth!" cried Agnes, suddenly. "It's at Mr. Bloomer's where Carrie Poole's having her big party cake made. Lucy told me so. Lucy is Carrie's cousin, you know."

"I heard about that party," said Tess. "It's going to be *grand*. Are you and Aggie going, Ruth?"

"I'm sure I don't know," said the oldest Corner House girl. "I haven't been invited yet."

"Nor me, either," confessed Agnes. "Don't you suppose we shall be? I want to go, awfully, Ruthie."

"It's the first really *big* party that's been gotten up this winter," agreed Ruth. "I don't know Carrie Poole very well, though she's in my class."

"They live in a great big farmhouse on the Buckshot Road," Agnes said. "Lucy told me. A beautiful place. Lots of the girls in my grade are going. Trix Severn is very good friends with Carrie Poole, they say. Why, Ruth! can *that* be the reason why we haven't been invited?"

"*What's* the reason?"

"'Cause Trix is good friends with Carrie? Trix's mother is some relation to Mrs. Poole. That Trix girl is so mean I *know* she'll just work us out of any invitation to the party."

Agnes' eyes flashed and it looked as though a storm was coming. But Ruth remained tranquil.

"There will be other parties," the older girl said. "It won't kill us to miss this one."

"Speak for yourself!" complained Agnes. "It just kill us with some of the girls. The Pooles are very select. If we are left out of Carrie's party, we'll be left out of the best of everything that goes on this winter."

Ruth would not admit to Agnes just how badly she felt about the fact that they were seemingly overlooked by Carrie Poole in the distribution of the latter's favors. The party was to be on the Friday night of the week immediately preceding Christmas.

There had been no snow of any consequence as yet, but plenty of cold weather. Milton Pond was safely frozen over and the Corner House girls were there almost every afternoon. Tess was learning to skate and Ruth and Agnes took turns drawing Dot about the pond on her sled.

Neale O'Neil had several furnaces to attend to now, and he always looked after the removal of the ashes to the curbline, and did other dirty work, immediately after school. But as soon as his work was finished he, too, hurried to the pond.

Neale was a favorite with the girls—and without putting forth any special effort on his part to be so. He was of a retiring disposition, and aside from his acquaintanceship with some of the boys of his grade and his friendship with the Corner House girls, Neale O'Neil did not appear to care much for youthful society.

For one thing, Neale felt his position keenly. He was the oldest scholar in his class. Miss Shipman considered him her brightest pupil, but the fact remained that he really should have been well advanced in high school. Ruth Kenway was only a year older than Neale.

His size, his good looks, and his graceful skating, attracted the attention of the older girls who sought the Milton Pond for recreation.

"There's that Neale O'Neil," said Carrie Poole, to some friends, on this particular afternoon, when she saw the boy putting on his skates. "Don't any of you girls know him? I want him at my party."

"He's dreadfully offish," complained Pearl Harrod.

"He seems to be friendly enough with the Corner House girls," said Carrie. "If they weren't such stuck-up things—"

"Who says they're stuck up?" demanded her cousin Lucy. "I'm sure Aggie isn't."

"Trix says she is. And I must say Ruth keeps to herself a whole lot. She's in my class but I scarcely ever speak to her," said Carrie.

"Now you've said something," laughed Eva Larry. "Ruth isn't a girl who puts herself forward, believe me!"

"They're all four jolly girls," declared Lucy.

"The kids and all."

"Oh! I don't want any kids out to the house Friday night," said Carrie.

"Do you mean to say you haven't asked Aggie and Ruth?" gasped Pearl.

"Not yet."

"Why not?" demanded Lucy, bluntly.

"Why—I don't know them very well," said Carrie, hastily. "But I *do* want that Neale O'Neil. So few boys know how to act at a party. And I wager *he* dances."

"I can tell you right now," said Lucy, "you'll never get him to come unless the Corner House girls are invited. Why! they're the only girls of us all who know him right well."

"I am going to try him," said Carrie Poole, with sudden decision.

She skated right over to Neale O'Neil just as he had finished strapping on the cobbler's old skates that had been lent him. Carrie Poole was a big girl—nearly seventeen. She was too wise to attack Neale directly with the request she had to make.

"Mr. O'Neil," she said, with a winning smile, "I saw you doing the 'double-roll' the other day, and you did it so easily! I've been trying to get it for a long while. Will you show me—please—just a little?"

Even the gruffest boy could scarcely escape from such a net—and Neale O'Neil was never impolite. He agreed to show her, and did so. Of course they became more or less friendly within a few minutes.

"It's so kind of you," said Carrie, when she had managed to get the figure very nicely. "I'm a thousand times obliged. But it wasn't just this that I wanted to talk with you about."

Neale looked amazed. He was not used to the feminine mind.

"I wanted to pluck up my courage," laughed Carrie, "to ask you to come to my party Friday evening. Just a lot of the boys and girls, all of whom you know, I am sure. I'd dearly love to have you come, Mr. O'Neil."

"But—but I don't really know *your* name," stammered Neale.

"Why! I'm Carrie Poole."

"And I'm sure I don't know where you live," Neale hastened to say. "It's very kind of you—"

"Then you'll come?" cried Carrie, confidently. "We live out of town—on the Buckshot Road. Anybody will tell you."

"I suppose the Kenway girls will know," said Neale, doubtfully. "I can go along with them."

Carrie was a girl who thought quickly. She had really promised Trix Severn that she would not invite Ruth and Agnes Kenway to her party; but how could she get out of doing just that under these circumstances?

"Of course," she cried, with apparently perfect frankness. "I sincerely hope they'll both come. And I can depend upon you to be there, Mr. O'Neil?"

Then she skated straight away and found Ruth and Agnes and invited them for Friday night in a most graceful way.

"I wanted to ask you girls personally instead of sending a formal invite," she said, warmly. "You being new girls, you know. You'll come? That's so kind of you! I shouldn't feel that the party would be a success if you Corner House girls were not there."

So that is how they got the invitation; but at the time the Kenway sisters did not suspect how near they came to not being invited at all to the Christmas party.

CHAPTER XIII

THE BARN DANCE

Such a "hurly-burly" as there was about the old Corner House on Friday afternoon! Everybody save Aunt Sarah was on the *qui vive* over the Christmas party—for this was the first important social occasion to which any of the Kenway sisters had been invited since coming to Milton to live.

Miss Titus, that famous gossip and seamstress, had been called in again, and the girls all had plenty of up-to-date winter frocks made. Miss Titus' breezy conversation vastly interested Dot, who often sat silently nursing her Alice-doll in the sewing room, ogling the seamstress wonderingly as her tongue ran on. "'N so, you see, he says to her," was a favorite phrase with Miss Titus.

Mrs. MacCall said the seamstress' tongue was "hung in the middle and ran at both ends." But Dot's comment was even more to the point. After Miss Titus had started home after a particularly gossipy day at the old Corner House, Dot said:

"Ruthie, don't you think Miss Titus seems to know an awful lot of *un-so news*?"

However, to come to the important Friday of Carrie Poole's

party: Ruth and Agnes were finally dressed. They only *looked* at their supper. Who wanted to eat just before going to a real, country barn-dance? That is what Carrie had promised her school friends.

Ruth and Agnes had their coats and furs on half an hour before Neale O'Neil came for them. It was not until then that the girls noticed how really shabby Neale was. His overcoat was thin, and plainly had not been made for him.

Ruth knew she could not give the proud boy anything of value. He was making his own way and had refused every offer of assistance they had made him. He bore his poverty jauntily and held his head so high, and looked at the world so fearlessly, that it would have taken courage indeed to have accused him of being in need.

He strutted along beside the girls, his unmittened hands deep in his pockets. His very cheerfulness denied the cold, and when Ruth timidly said something about it, Neale said gruffly that "mittens were for babies!"

It was a lowery evening as the trio of young folk set forth. The clouds had threatened snow all day, and occasionally a flake—spying out the land ahead of its vast army of brothers—drifted through the air and kissed one's cheek.

Ruth, Agnes, and Neale talked of the possible storm, and the coming Christmas season, and of school, as they hurried along. It was a long walk out the Buckshot Road until they came in sight of the brilliantly lighted Poole farmhouse.

It stood at the top of the hill—a famous coasting place—and it looked almost like a castle, with all its windows alight, and now and then a flutter of snowflakes falling between the approaching young people and the lampshine from the doors and windows.

The girls and boys were coming from all directions—some from across the open, frozen fields, some from crossroads, and other groups, like the Corner House girls and Neale O'Neil, along the main highway.

Some few came in hacks, or private carriages; but not many. Milton people were, for the most part, plain folk, and frowned upon any ostentation.

The Corner House girls and their escort reached the Poole homestead in good season. The entire lower floor was open to them, save the kitchen, where Mother Poole and the hired help were busy with the huge supper that was to be served later.

There was music and singing, and a patheoscope entertainment at first, while everybody was getting acquainted with everybody else. But the boys soon escaped to the barn.

The Poole barn was an enormous one. The open floor, with the great mows on either side, and the forest of rafters overhead, could have accommodated a full company of the state militia, for its drill and evolutions.

Under the mows on either hand were the broad stalls for the cattle—the horses' intelligent heads looking over the mangers at the brilliantly lighted scene, from one side, while the mild-eyed cows and oxen chewed their cud on the other side of the barn floor.

All the farm machinery and wagons had been removed, and the open space thoroughly swept. Rows of Chinese lanterns, carefully stayed so that the candles should not set them afire, were strung from end to end of the barn. Overhead the beams of three great lanterns were reflected downward upon the dancing-floor.

When the boys first began to crowd out to the barn, all the decorating was not quite finished, and the workmen had left a rope hanging from a beam above. Some of the boys began swinging on that rope.

"Here's Neale! Here's Neale O'Neil!" cried one of the sixth grade boys when Neale appeared. "Come on, Neale. Show us what you did on the rope in the school gym."

Most boys can easily be tempted to "show off" a little when it comes to gymnastic exercises. Neale seized the rope and began to mount it, stiff-legged and "hand over hand." It was a feat that a professional acrobat would have found easy, but that very few but professionals could have accomplished.

It was when he reached the beam that the boy surprised his mates. He got his legs over the beam and rested for a moment; then he commenced the descent.

In some way he wrapped his legs around the rope and, head down, suddenly shot toward the floor at a fear-exciting pace.

Several of the girls, with Mr. Poole, were just entering the barn. The girls shrieked, for they thought Neale was falling.

But the boy halted in midflight, swung up his body quickly, seized the rope again with both hands, and dropped lightly to the floor.

"Bravo!" cried Mr. Poole, leading the applause. "I declare, that was well done. I saw a boy at Twomley & Sorber's Circus this last summer do that very thing—and he did it no better."

"Oh, but that couldn't have been Neale, Mr. Poole," Agnes Kenway hastened to say, "for Neale tells us that he never went to a circus in his life."

"He might easily be the junior member of an acrobatic troupe, just the same," said Mr. Poole; but Neale had slipped away from them for the time being and the farmer got no chance to interview the boy.

A large-sized talking machine was wheeled into place and the farmer put in the dance records himself. The simple dances—such as they had learned at school or in the juvenile dancing classes—brought even the most bashful boys out upon the floor. There were no wallflowers, for Carrie was a good hostess and, after all, had picked her company with some judgment.

The girls began dancing with their furs and coats on; but soon they threw their wraps aside, for the barn floor seemed as warm as any ballroom.

They had lots of fun in the "grand march," and with a magic-lantern one of the boys flashed vari-colored lights upon the crowd from the loft-ladder at the end of the barn.

Suddenly Mr. Poole put a band record in the machine, and as the march struck up, the great doors facing the house were rolled back. They had been dancing for more than two hours. It was after ten o 'clock.

"Oh!" shouted the girls.

"Ah!" cried the boys.

The snow was now drifting steadily down, and between the illumination by the colored slides in the lantern, and that from the blazing windows of the big house, it was indeed a scene to suggest fairyland!

"Into the house—all of you!" shouted Mr. Poole. "Boys, assist your partners through the snow."

"Come on! Come on!" shouted Carrie, in the lead with Neale O'Neil. "Forward, the Light Brigade!"

"Charge for the *eats*, they said!" added Agnes. "Oh—ow—ouch! over my shoe in the snow."

"And it's we-e-e-et!" wailed another of the girls. "Right down my neck!"

"'Be-you-ti-ful snow! He may sing whom it suits—
I object to the stuff 'cause it soaks through my boots!'"

quoted Agnes. "Hurry up, you ahead!"

So the march was rather ragged—more in the nature of a raid, indeed. But they had to halt at the side door where the two maids stood armed with brooms, for Mrs. Poole did not propose that the crowd should bring in several bushels of snow on their feet.

In the dining and sitting-rooms were long tables, and all loaded with good things. There were no seats, but plenty of standing room about the tables. Everybody helped everybody else, and there was a lot of fun.

Some of the girls began to be troubled by the storm. They made frequent trips to the windows to look out of doors. Soon wraps appeared and the girls began to say good-night to their young hostess.

"I don't see how we're ever going to get home!" cried one of the girls who lived at the greatest distance.

Farmer Poole had thought of that. He had routed out his men again, and they harnessed the horses to a big pung and to two smaller sleighs.

Into these vehicles piled both boys and girls who lived on the other side of Milton. A few private equipages arrived for some of the young folk. The fathers of some had tramped through the snow to the farmhouse to make sure that their daughters were properly escorted home in the fast quickening storm.

To look out of doors, it seemed a perfect wall of falling snow that the lamplight streamed out upon. Fortunately it was not very cold, nor did the wind blow. But at the corner of the house there was a drift as deep as Neale O'Neil's knees.

"But we'll pull through all right, girls, if you want to try it," he assured Ruth and Agnes.

They did not like to wait until the sledges got back; that might not be for an hour. And even then the vehicles would be overcrowded. "Come on!" said Agnes. "Let's risk it, Ruth."

"I don't know but that we'd better—"

"Pshaw! Neale will get us through. He knows a shortcut—so he says."

"Of course we can trust Neale," said the older Corner House girl, smiling, and she made no further objection.

They had already bidden their hostess and her father and

mother good-night. So when the trio set off toward town nobody saw them start. They took the lane beside the barn and went right down the hill, between the stone fences, now more than half hidden by the snow.

When they got upon the flats, and the lights of the house were hidden, it did seem as though they were in a great, white desert.

"Who told you this was a short way to town?" demanded Agnes, of Neale.

"Why, one of the girls told me," Neale said, innocently enough. "You know—that Severn girl."

"What! Trix Severn?" shrieked Agnes.

"Yes."

"I believe she started you off this way, just for the sake of getting us all into trouble," cried Agnes. "Let's go back!"

But they were now some distance out upon the flats. Far, far ahead there were faint lights, denoting the situation of Milton; but behind them all the lights on the hill had been quenched. The Pooles had extinguished the lamps at the back of the house, and of course ere this the great barn itself was shrouded in darkness.

The snow came thicker and faster. They were in the midst of a world of white and had there been any shelter at all at hand, Neale would have insisted upon taking advantage of it. But there was nothing of the kind.

CHAPTER XIV

UNCLE RUFUS' STORY OF THE CHRISTMAS GOOSE

"Trix is going to stay all night with Carrie. If we go back she will only laugh at us," Ruth Kenway said, decidedly.

"We-ell," sighed Agnes. "I don't want to give that mean thing a chance to laugh. We can't really get lost out here, can we, Neale?"

"I don't see how we can," said Neale, slowly. "I'm game to go ahead if you girls are."

"It looks to me just as bad to go back," Ruth observed.

"Come on!" cried Agnes, and started forward again through the snow.

And, really, they might just as well keep on as to go back. They must be half way to the edge of Milton by this time, all three were sure.

The "swish, swish, swish" of the slanting snow was all they heard save their own voices. The falling particles deadened all sound, and they might have been alone in a wilderness as far as the presence of other human beings was made known to them.

"Say!" grumbled Neale, "she said there was a brook here somewhere—at the bottom of a hollow."

"Well, we've been going down hill for some time," Ruth remarked. "It must be near by now."

"Is—isn't there a—a bridge over it?" quavered Agnes.

"A culvert that we can walk over," said Neale. "Let me go ahead. Don't you girls come too close behind me."

"But, goodness, Neale!" cried Agnes. "We mustn't lose sight of you."

"I'm not going to run away from you."

"But you're the last boy on earth—as far as we can see," chuckled Agnes. "You have suddenly become very precious."

Neale grinned. "Get you once to the old Corner House and neither of you would care if you didn't ever see a boy again," he said.

He had not gone on five yards when the girls, a few paces behind, heard him suddenly shout. Then followed a great splashing and floundering about.

"Oh! oh! Neale!" shrieked Agnes. "Have you gone under?"

"No! But I've gone through," growled the boy. "I've busted through a thin piece of ice. Here's the brook all right; you girls stay where you are. I can see the culvert."

He came back to them, sopping wet to his knees. In a few moments the lower part of his limbs and his feet were encased in ice.

"You'll get your death of cold, Neale," cried Ruth, worriedly.

"No, I won't, Ruth. Not if I keep moving. And that's what we'd all better do. Come on," the boy said. "I know the way after we cross this brook. There is an unfinished street leads right into town. Comes out there by your store building— where those Italian kids live."

"Oh! If Mrs. Kranz should be up," gasped Agnes, "she'd take us in and let you dry your feet, Neale."

"We'll get her up," declared Ruth. "She's as good-hearted as she can be, and she won't mind."

"But it's midnight," chattered Neale, beginning to feel the chill.

They hurried over the culvert and along the rough street. Far ahead there was an arc light burning on the corner of Meadow Street. But not a soul was astir in the neighborhood as the trio came nearer to the German woman's grocery store, and the corner where Joe Maroni, the father of Maria, had his vegetable and fruit stand.

The Italians were all abed in their miserable quarters below the street level; but there was a lamp alight behind the shade of Mrs. Kranz's sitting room. Agnes struggled ahead through the drifts and the falling snow, and tapped at the window.

There were startled voices at once behind the blind. The window had a number of iron bars before it and was supposed to be burglar-proof. Agnes tapped again, and then the shade moved slightly.

"Go avay! Dere iss noddings for you here yedt!" exclaimed Mrs. Kranz, threateningly. "Go avay, or I vill de berlice call."

They saw her silhouette on the blind. But there was another shadow, too, and when this passed directly between the lamp and the window, the girls saw that it was Maria Maroni. Maria often helped Mrs. Kranz about the house, and sometimes remained with her all night.

"Oh, Maria! Maria Maroni!" shrieked Agnes, knocking on the pane again. "Let us in—*do*!"

The Italian girl flew to the window and ran up the shade, despite the expostulations of Mrs. Kranz, who believed that the party outside were troublesome young folk of the neighborhood.

But when she knew who they were—and Maria identified them immediately—the good lady lumbered to the side door of the store herself, and opened it wide to welcome Ruth and Agnes, with their boy friend.

"Coom in! Coom in by mine fire," she cried. "Ach! der poor kinder oudt in dis vedder yedt. Idt iss your deaths mit cold you vould catch—no?"

Ruth explained to the big-hearted German widow how they came to be struggling in the storm at such an hour.

"Undt dot boy iss vet? Ach! Ledt him his feet dake off qvick! Maria! make de chocolate hot. Undt de poy—ach! I haf somedings py mine closet in, for *him*."

She bustled away to reappear in a moment with a tiny glass of something that almost strangled Neale when he drank it, but, as he had to admit, "it warmed 'way down to the ends of his toes!"

"Oh, this is *fine!*" Agnes declared, ten minutes later, when she was sipping her hot chocolate. "I *love* the snow—and this was almost like getting lost in a blizzard."

Mrs. Kranz shook her head. "Say nodt so—say nodt so," she rumbled. "Dis iss pad yedt for de poor folk. Yah! idt vill make de coal go oop in brice."

"Yes," said Maria, softly. "My papa says he will have to charge twelve cents a pail for coal to-morrow, instead of ten. He has to pay more."

"I never thought of *that* side of it," confessed Agnes, slowly. "I suppose a snow storm like this *will* make it hard for poor people."

"Undt dere iss blenty poor folk all about us," said Mrs. Kranz, shaking her head. "Lucky you are, dot you know noddings about idt."

"Why shouldn't we know something about it?" demanded Ruth, quickly. "Do you mean there will be much suffering among *our* tenants because of this storm, Mrs. Kranz?"

"Gott sie dank! nodt for *me*," said the large lady, shaking her head. "Undt not for Maria's fadder. Joe Maroni iss doin' vell. But many are nodt so—no. Undt der kinder—"

"Let's give them all a Christmas," exclaimed Ruth, having a sudden bright, as well as kind, thought. "I'll ask Mr. Howbridge. You shall tell us of those most in need, Mrs.

Kranz—you and Maria."

"Vell dem poor Goronofskys iss de vorst," declared the grocery-store woman, shaking her head.

Ruth and Agnes remembered the reported riches in Sadie Goronofsky's bank, but although they looked at each other, they said nothing about it.

"Sadie has an awful hard time," said Maria.

"De sthep-mudder does nodt treat her very kindly—Oh, I know! She has so many kinder of her own. Sadie vork all de time ven she iss de school oudt."

They discussed the other needy neighbors for half an hour longer. Then Neale put on his dried shoes and stockings, tied his trouser-legs around his ankles, and announced himself ready to go. The girls were well protected to their knees by leggings, so they refused to remain for the night at Mrs. Kranz's home.

They set out bravely to finish their journey to the old Corner House. Some of the drifts were waist deep and the wind had begun to blow. "My! but I'm glad we're not over on those flats now," said Agnes.

It was almost one o'clock when they struggled through the last drift and reached the back door of the old Corner House. Uncle Rufus, his feet on the stove-hearth, was sleeping in his old armchair, waiting up for them.

"Oh, Uncle Rufus! you ought to be abed," cried Ruth.

"You've lost your beauty sleep, Uncle Rufus," added Agnes.

"Sho', chillen, dis ain't nottin' fo' ol' Unc' Rufus. He sit up many a night afore dis. An' somebody has ter watch de Christmas goose."

"Oh! The Christmas goose?" cried Agnes. "Has it come?"

"You wanter see him, chillen?" asked the old colored man, shuffling to the door. "Looker yere."

They followed him to the woodshed door. There, roosting on one leg and blinking at them in the lamplight, was a huge gray goose. It hissed softly at them, objecting to their presence, and they went back into the warm kitchen.

"Why does it stand that way—on one leg—Uncle Rufus?" asked Agnes.

"Perhaps it's resting the other foot," Ruth said, laughing.

"Maybe it has only one leg," Neale observed.

At that Uncle Rufus began chuckling enormously to himself. His eyes rolled, and his cheeks "blew out," and he showed himself to be very "tickled."

The door latch clicked and here appeared Tess and Dot in their warm robes and slippers. They had managed to wake up when the big girls and Neale came in, and had now stolen down to hear about the party.

Mrs. MacCall had left a nice little lunch, and a pot of cocoa to warm them up. The girls gathered their chairs in a half circle about the front of the kitchen range, with Neale, and while Uncle Rufus got the refreshments ready, Ruth and Agnes told their sisters something about the barn dance.

But Neale had his eye on the old colored man. "What's the matter, Uncle?" he asked. "What's amusing you so much?"

"I done been t'inkin' ob 'way back dar befo' de wah—yas-sir. I done been t'inkin' ob das Christmas goose—he! he! he! das de funniest t'ing—"

"Oh, tell us about it, Uncle Rufus!" cried Ruth.

"Do tell us," added Agnes, "for we're not a bit sleepy yet."

"Make room for Uncle Rufus' armchair," commanded Ruth. "Come, Uncle Rufus: we're ready."

Nothing loath the old fellow settled into his creaking chair and looked into the glowing coals behind the grated fire-box door.

"Disher happen' befo' de wah," he said, slowly. "I warn't mo' dan a pickerninny—jes' knee-high to a mus'rat, as yo' might say. But I kin member ol' Mars' Colby's plantation de bery yeah befo' de wah.

"Well, chillen, as I was sayin', disher Christmas I kin 'member lak' it was yestidy. My ol' mammy was de sho' 'nuff cook at de big house, an' Mars' Colby t'ought a heap ob her. But she done tuk down wid de mis'ry in her back jes' two days fore Christmas—an' de big house full ob comp'ny!

"Sech a gwine 'bout yuh nebber *did* see, w'en mammy say she couldn't cook de w'ite folkses' dinner. Dere was a no-'count yaller gal, Sally Alley dey call her, wot he'ped erbout de breakfas' an' sech; but she warn't a sho' 'nuff cook—naw'm!

"She 'lowed she was. She was de beatenes' gal for t'inkin' she knowed eberyt'ing. But, glo-*ree*! dar wasn't nobody on dat plantation wot could cook er goose tuh suit Mars' Colby lak' my ol' mammy.

"And de goose dey'd picked out fo' dat Christmas dinner sho' was a noble bird—ya-as'm! Dere was an army ob geese aroun' de pond, but de one dey'd shet up fo' two weeks, an' fed soft fodder to wid er spoon, was de noblest ob de ban'," said Uncle Rufus, unctuously.

"Well, dar warn't time tuh send on to Richmon' fo' a sho' 'nuff cook, an' de dinnah pahty was gaddered togedder. So Mars' Colby had ter let dat uppity yaller gal go ahead an' do her worstest.

"She sho' done it," said Uncle Rufus, shaking his head. "Dar nebber was sech anudder dinner sarbed on de Colby table befo' dat time, nor, since.

"My mammy, a-layin' on her back in de quahtahs, an' groanin', sent me up to de big house kitchen tuh watch. I was big 'nuff to he'p mammy, and it was in dat kitchen I begin ter l'arn ter be a house sarbent.

"Well, chillen, I kep' my two eyes open, an' I sabed de sauce from burnin', an' de roun' 'taters from bilin' over, an' de onions from sco'chin' an' de sweet-er-taters f'om bein' charcoal on one side an' baked raw on de odder. Glo-*ree*! dat was one 'citin' day in dat kitchen.

"But I couldn't sabe de goose from bein' sp'ilt. Dat was beyon' my powah. An' it happen disher way:

"De yaller gal git de goose all stuffed an' fixed propah, fo' she done use my mammy's resate fo' stuffin'. But de no-'count critter set it right down in de roastin' pan on de flo' by de po'ch door. Eroun' come snuffin' a lean houn' dawg, one ob de re'l ol' 'nebber-git enuff' breed. He's empty as er holler stump—er, he! he! he!" chuckled Uncle Rufus. "Glo-*ree*! dar allus was a slather of sech houn's aroun' dat plantation, fo' Mars' Colby was a fox huntah.

"Dat dawg git his eye on dat goose for jes' a secon'—an' de nex' secon' he grab hit by de laig!"

"Lawsy me! My soul an' body!" chortled Uncle Rufus, rocking himself to and fro in his chair in an ecstasy of enjoyment. "How dem niggers did squeal! Dar was more'n 'nuff boys an' gals 'roun' undah foot at dat time, but none ob dem git near de fracas but Unc' Rufus—naw'm!"

"My goodness! the dog didn't get away with the goose, did he, Uncle Rufus?" asked Ruth."

"I's a-comin' tuh dat—I's a-comin' tuh dat," repeated the old man. "I seen de goose gwine out de do', an' I grab hit—I sho' did! I grab it by de two wingses, an' I hang on liker chigger. De odder pickaninnies jes' a jumpin' eroun' an er-hollerin'. But Unc' Rufus knowed better'n *dat*.

"Dat houn' dawg, he pull, an' I pull, an' it sho' a wondah we didn' pull dat bird all apaht betwixt us. But erbout de secon' wrench dat hongry beast gib, he pull de laig clean off'n dat ol' goose!

"Glo-*ree*!" chuckled Uncle Rufus, rolling his eyes and weaving back and forth on his chair, in full enjoyment of his own story. "Glo-*ree*! Dat is a 'casion I ain't nebber lak'ly tuh fo'git. Dar I was on my back on de kitchen flo', wid de goose on top ob me, w'ile de houn'-dawg beat it erway from dar er mile-er-minit—ya-as'm!

"Dat yaller gal jerked dat goose out'n my arms an' put hit back in de pan, an clapped de pan inter de oven. 'Wedder hit's got one laig, or two,' says she, 'dat's de onliest one de w'ite folkses has got fo' dey's dinner."

"An dat was true 'nuff—true 'nuff," said Uncle Rufus. "But I begin tuh wondah wot Mars' Colby say 'bout dat los' laig? He was right quick wid hes temper, an' w'en hes mad was up— Glo-*ree*! he made de quahtahs *hot*! I wondah wot he do to dat yaller gal w'en dat raggedty goose come on de table.

"It done got cooked to a tu'n—ya-as! I nebber see a browner, nor a plumper goose. An' w'en dat Sally Alley done lay him on hes side, wid de los' laig *down*, hit was jes' a pitcher—jes' a pitcher!" declared Uncle Rufus, reminiscent yet of the long past feast-day.

"Wal, dar warn't ne'der ob de waitresses willin' tuh tak' dat goose in an' put it down befo' Mars' Colby—naw'm! So dat yaller gal had to put on a clean han'kercher an' ap'on, an' do it her own se'f. I was jes' leetle 'nuff so I crope th'u de do' an' hides behin' de co'nah ob de sidebo'd.

"I was moughty cur'ous," confessed Uncle Rufus. "I wanted tuh know jes' wot Mars' Colby say w'en he fin' dat goose ain' got but one laig on him."

"And what did he say, Uncle Rufus?" asked Agnes, breath-less with interest like the other listeners.

"Das is wot I is a-comin' to. You be patient, chile," chuckled Uncle Rufus.

"Dar was de long table, all set wid shinin' silber, an' glistenin' cut glass, an' de be-you-ti-ful ol' crockery dat Madam Colby—das Mars' Colby's gre't-gran-mammy—brought f'om

Englan'. Dar was ten plates beside de famb'ly.

"De waitresses am busy, a-flyin' eroun' wid de side dishes, an' Mis' Colby, she serbs at her side ob de table, w'en Mars' Colby, he get up tuh carve.

"'Wot paht ob de goose is yo' mos' fon' of, Miss Lee?' he say to de young lady on hes right han', monst'ous perlite lak."

"'I'd lak' a slice ob de laig, Cunnel,' she say; 't'ank yo'.'"

Uncle Rufus was surely enjoying himself. He was imitating "the quality" with great gusto. His eyes rolled, his sides shook, and his brown face was all one huge smile.

"De bery nex' lady he ax dat same question to, mak' de same reply," went on Uncle Rufus, "an' Mars' Colby done cut all de laig meat erway on dat side. Den it come ergin. Somebody else want er piece ob de secon' j'int.

"Mars' Colby stick his fo'k in de goose an' heave him over in de plattah. Glo-*ree*! dar de under side ob dat goose were all nice an' brown; but dar warn't no sign ob a laig erpon hit!

"'Wha' dis? Wha' dis?' Mars' Colby cry. 'Who been a-tamperin' wid dis goose? Sen' dat no-'count Sally Alley in yeah dis minute!' he say to one ob de waitresses.

"Glo-*ree*! how scar't we all was. My knees shak' tergedder, an' I bit my tongue tryin' ter hol' my jaws shet. W'en Mars' Colby done let loose—well!" and Uncle Rufus sighed.

"Den dey come back wid Sally Alley. If eber dar was a scar't nigger on dat plantation, it was dat same yaller gal. An' she warn't saddle color no mo'; she was grayer in de face dan an ol' rat.

"Dey stan' her up befo' Mars' Colby, an' hes eyes look lak' dey was red—ya-as'm! 'Sally Alley,' he roar at her, 'whar de odder laig ob dis goose?'

"Sally Alley shake like a willer by de ribber, an' she blurt out: 'Mars' Colby! sho' 'nuff dar warn't no odder laig *on* dat goose.'"

"'Wha' dat?' say he, moughty savage. 'On'y *one* laig on dis goose?'"

"'Ya-as, suh—sho' 'nuff. Das de onliest laig it had,' says she."

"'What do yo' mean?' Mars' Colby cry. 'Yo' tell me my goose ain' hab but one laig?'"

"'Ya-as, suh. Das hit. On'y one laig,' says dat scar't yaller gal, an' ter clinch it she added, '*All* yo' geese dat a-ways, Mars' Colby. Dey all ain' got but one laig.'"

"Oh!" squealed Dot.

"Was it sure enough *so*, Uncle Rufus?" asked Tess, in awe.

"Yo' wait! yo' wait, chillen! I'se gittin' tuh dat," declared the old man, chuckling. "Co'se dat Sally Alley say dat, hysterical lak'. She was dat scar't. Mars' Colby scowl at her mo' awful.

"'I mak' yo' prove dat to me atter dinner,' he say, savage as he kin be. 'Yo'll tak' us all out dar an' show us my one-laiged geese. An' if it *ain't* so, I'll send yo' to de fiel' oberseer.'"

"De fiel' oberseer do de whippin' on dat plantation," whispered Uncle Rufus, "an' Sally Alley knowed wot dat meant."

"Oh, dear me!" cried tender-hearted Tess. "They didn't re'lly *beat* her?"

"Don't try to get ahead of the story, Tess," said Agnes, but rather shakingly. "We'll all hear it together."

"Das it," said Uncle Rufus. "Jes' gib Unc' Rufus time an' he'll tell it all. Dat yaller gal sho' was in a fix. She don' know w'ich way to tu'n.

"Das dinner was a-gettin' nearer an' nearer to de en'. Mars' Colby do lak' he say den. He come out an' mak' Sally Alley show de one-laiged geese.

"'I has a po'erful min',' dat Sally gal say, 'ter go down dar an' chop er laig off'n ebery goose in de yard.'"

"But she didn't hab no min' to do dat," pursued Uncle Rufus. "Naw'm. She didn't hab no min' for nottin', she was dat flabbergastuated.

"She t'ink she run erway; but she wouldn't git far befo' Mars' Colby be atter her wid de houn's. Dar ain't no place to run to, an' she ain't got no mammy, so she run tuh mine," said Uncle Rufus, shaking his head. "An' my mammy was a wise ol' woman. She done been bawn in de Colby famb'ly, an' she know Mars' Colby better dan he know he'self. Fiery as he was, she know dat if yo' kin mak' him laff, he'd fo'give a nigger 'most anyt'ing.

"So my ol' mammy tol' Sally Alley wot tuh say an' do. Sally wipe her eyes an' mak' herse'f neat erg'in, an' wa'k up ter de big house brave as a lion—in de seemin'—jes' as de gran' folkses comes out upon de lawn.

"'Here, yo',' 'sclaim Mars' Colby, we'n he see her. 'Yo' come an' show me all dem one-laiged geese.'"

"'Ya-as, Mars',' says Sally Alley, an' she haid right off fo' de goose pon'. Dar was de whole flock roostin' erlong de aidge ob de pon'—an' all wid one foot drawed up in deir fedders lak' dat goose roostin' out dar in dat woodshed dis bressed minute!

"'Wot I tell yo'? Wot I tell yo', Mars' Colby?' cry Sally Alley. 'Ain't all dem gooses got one laig lak' I tol' yo'?'"

"But Mars' stride right ober to de fence an' clap hes han's. Ebery one o' dem geese puts down hes foot an' tu'ns to look at him."

"'Das ain' no fair! das ain' no fair, Mars' Colby!' squeals dat yaller gal, all 'cited up. *Yo' didn't clap yo' han's at dat goose on de table!*'—er, he! he! he!" And so Uncle Rufus finished the story of the Christmas goose.

Ruth started the younger ones to bed immediately; but Tess called down from the stair:

"Uncle Rufus! He *didn't* make her go see the field overseer, did he?"

"Sho'ly not, chile. Dat wasn' Cunnel Mark Colby's way. My ol' mammy knowed wot would han'le him. He done give one big laff, an' sent Sally Alley off to Aunt Jinny, de house-keeper, tuh cut her off a new kaliker dress pattern. But dem quality folkses sho' was tickled erbout dat one-laiged goose."

CHAPTER XV

SADIE GORONOFSKY'S BANK

When Ruth Kenway had an idea—a real *good* idea—it usually bore fruit. She had evolved one of her very best that snowy night while she and Agnes and Neale O'Neil were drinking hot chocolate in Mrs. Kranz's parlor.

It was impossible for Ruth to get downtown on Saturday. One reason was, they all got up late, having crept into bed at half-past four. Then, there were the usual household tasks, for all four of the Corner House girls had their established duties on Saturday.

The streets were so full of snow that it would have been almost impossible for Ruth to have gotten to Mr. Howbridge's office then; but she went there Monday afternoon.

Mr. Howbridge had been Uncle Peter Stower's lawyer, and it was he who had brought the news to the four Kenway girls when they lived in Bloomingsburg, that they were actually rich.

He was a tall, gray gentleman, with sharp eyes and a beaklike nose, and he looked wonderfully stern and implacable unless he smiled. But he always had a smile for Ruth Kenway.

The lawyer had acquired a very deep respect for Ruth's good sense and for her character in general. As he said, there were so many narrow, stingy souls in the world, it was refreshing to meet a generous nature like that of the oldest Corner House girl.

"And what is it now, Miss Ruth?" asked the gentleman when she entered his private office, and shaking hands with her. "Have you come to consult me professionally, or am I honored by a social call?"

"You are almost the best man who ever lived, Mr. Howbridge," laughed Ruth. "I *know* you are the best guardian, for you let me do mostly just as I please. So I am confident you are going to grant *this* request—"

Mr. Howbridge groaned. "You are beginning in your usual way, I see," he said. "You want something of me—but it is for somebody else you want it, I'll be bound."

"Oh, no, sir! it is really for me," declared Ruth. "I'd like quite some money."

"What for, may I ask?"

"Of course, sir. I've come to consult you about it. You see, it's the tenants."

"Those Meadow Street people!" exclaimed the lawyer. "Your Uncle Peter made money out of them; and his father did before him. But my books will show little profit from those houses at the end of this year—of that I am sure."

"But, if we have made so much out of the houses in the past, shouldn't we spend some of the profit on the tenants *now*?" asked Ruth earnestly.

"You are the most practical *im*practical person I ever met," declared Mr. Howbridge, laughing rather ruefully.

Ruth did not just understand that; but she was much in earnest and she put before the lawyer the circumstances of some of the tenants of the old houses on Meadow Street, as she had heard them from Mrs. Kranz and Maria Maroni.

She did not forget the Goronofskys, despite Tess' story of Sadie's bank in which she was saving her Christmas money; but she did not mention this last to the lawyer.

Ruth wanted of the lawyer details of all the families on the estate's books. She wished to know the earning capacity of each family, how they lived, the number of children in each, and their ages and sex.

"You see, Mr. Howbridge, a part of our living—and it is a good living—comes from these people. We girls should know more about them. And I am anxious to do something for them this Christmas—especially for the little children."

"Well, I suppose I shall give in to you; but my better judgment cries out against it, Miss Ruth," declared the lawyer. "You see Perkins—my clerk. He collects the rents and knows all the tenants. I believe he knows when each man gets paid, how much he gets, and all about it. And, of course, as you say, you'll want some money."

"Yes, sir. This is for all of us—all four of us Corner House girls. Agnes, and Tess, and Dot, are just as anxious to help these people as I am. I am sure, Mr. Howbridge, whatever else you may do with money of the estate, *this* expense will never be questioned by any of us."

From Mrs. Kranz and Perkins, Ruth obtained the information

that she wished. The Corner House girls knew they could do no great thing; but for the purchase of small presents that children would appreciate, the twenty-five dollars Ruth got from Mr. Perkins, would go a long way.

And what fun the Corner House girls had doing that shopping! Tess and Dot did their part, and that the entire five and ten cent store was not bought out was not *their* fault.

"You can get such a lot for your money in that store," Dot gravely announced, "that a dollar seems twice as big as it does anywhere else."

"But I don't want the other girls to think we are just 'ten-centers,'" Agnes said. "Trix Severn says she wouldn't be seen going into such a cheap place."

"What do you care what people call you?" asked Ruth. "If you had been born in Indiana they'd have called you a 'Hoosier'; and if in North Carolina, they'd call you a 'Tar Heel.'"

"Or, if you were from Michigan, they'd say you were a 'Michigander,'" chuckled Neale, who was with them. "In *your* case, Aggie, it would be 'Michigoose.'"

"Is that so?" demanded Agnes, to whom Neale had once confessed that he was born in the state of Maine. "Then I suppose we ought to call *you* a 'Maniac,' eh?"

"Hit! a palpable hit!" agreed Neale, good-naturedly. "Come on! let's have some of your bundles. For goodness' sake! why didn't you girls bring a bushel basket—or engage a pack-mule?"

"We seem to have secured a very good substitute for the

latter," said Ruth, demurely.

All this shopping was done early in Christmas week, for the Corner House girls determined to allow nothing to break into their own home Christmas Eve celebration. The tree in Tess' room at school was going to be lighted up on Thursday afternoon; but Wednesday the Kenway girls were all excused from school early and Neale drove them over to Meadow Street in a hired sleigh.

They stopped before the doors of the respective shops of Mrs. Kranz and Joe Maroni. Joe's stand was strung with gay paper flowers and greens. He had a small forest of Christmas trees he was selling, just at the corner.

"Good-a day! good-a day, leetla padrona!" was his welcome for Ruth, and he bowed very low before the oldest Kenway girl, whom he insisted upon considering the real mistress of the house in which he and his family lived.

The little remembrances the girls had brought for Joe's family—down to a rattle for the baby—delighted the Italian. Tess had hung a special present for Maria on the school tree; but that was a secret as yet.

They carried all the presents into Mrs. Kranz's parlor and then Neale drove away, leaving the four Corner House girls to play their parts of *Lady Bountiful* without his aid.

They had just sallied forth for their first visit when, out of the Stower tenement in which the Goronofskys lived, boiled a crowd of shrieking, excited children. Sadie Goronofsky was at their head and a man in a blue suit and the lettered cap of a gas collector seemed the rallying point of the entire savage little gang.

"Oh! what is the matter, Sadie?" cried Tess, running to the little Jewish girl's side.

"He's a thief! he's a gonnif! he's a thief!" shrieked Sadie, dragging at the man's coat. "He stole mine money. He's busted open mine bank and stoled all mine money!"

"That red bank in the kitchen?" asked Tess, wonderingly. "That one your mother put the quarter in every week for you?"

"Sure!" replied the excited Sadie. "My mother's out. I'm alone with the kids. In this man comes and robs mine bank—"

"What *is* the trouble?" asked Ruth of the man.

"Why, bless you, somebody's been fooling the kid," he said, with some compassion. "And it was a mean trick. They told her the quarter-meter was a bank and that all the money that was put in it should be hers.

"She's a good little kid, too. I've often seen her taking care of her brothers and sisters and doing the work. The meter had to be opened to-day and the money taken out—and she caught me at it."

Afterward Agnes said to Ruth: "I could have *hugged* that man, Ruthie—for he didn't laugh!"

CHAPTER XVI

A QUARTETTE OF LADY BOUNTIFULS

For once the stolid little Sadie was unfaithful to her charges. She forgot the little ones her step-mother had left in her care; but the neighbors looked out for them.

She stood upon the icy walk, when she understood the full truth about "the big red bank in the kitchen," and watched with tearless eyes the gas collector walk away.

Her face worked pitifully; her black eyes grew hot; but she would not let the tears fall. She clenched her little red hands, bit her lower lip, and stamped her worn shoe upon the walk. Hatred of all mankind—not alone of the woman who had so wickedly befooled her—was welling up in little Sadie Goronofsky's heart.

It was then that Ruth Kenway put her arm around the little Jewish girl's shoulders and led her away to Mrs. Kranz's back parlor. There the Corner House girls told her how sorry they were; Mrs. Kranz filled her hands with "coffee kringle." Then some of the very best of the presents the Corner House girls had brought were chosen for Sadie's brothers and sisters, and Sadie was to be allowed to take them home herself to them.

"I don't mind being guyed by the kids at school because I can't put nothin' on that old Christmas tree. But I been promisin' *her* kids they should each have suthin' fine. She's been foolin' them jest the same as she has me. I don't know what my papa ever wanted ter go and marry *her* for," concluded Sadie, with a sniff.

"Hey! hey!" exclaimed Mrs. Kranz, sternly. "Iss dot de vay to talk yedt about your mamma?"

"She ain't my mamma," declared Sadie, sullenly.

"Sthop dot, Sadie!" said Mrs. Kranz. "You cand't remember how sweedt your papa's wife was to you when you was little. Who do you s'pose nursed you t'rough de scarlet fever dot time? Idt wass her."

"Huh!" grunted Sadie, but she took a thoughtful bite of cake.

"Undt de measles, yedt," went on Mrs. Kranz. "Like your own mamma, she iss dot goot to you. But times iss hardt now, undt poor folks always haf too many babies."

"She don't treat me like she was my mamma now," complained Sadie, with a sob that changed to a hiccough as she sipped the mug of coffee that had been the accompaniment of the cake. "She hadn't ought to told me those quarters she put in that box was mine, when they was to pay the gas man."

Mrs. Kranz eyed the complainant shrewdly. "Why vor shouldt you pe paid vor he'pin' your mamma yedt?" she asked. "You vouldn't haf gone from school home yedt undt helped her, if it hadn't been for vat she toldt you about de money. You vorked for de money every time—aind't idt?"

Sadie hung her head.

"Dot is idt!" cried the good German woman. "You make your poor mamma tell things to fool you, else you vould sthay avay an' blay. She haf to bribe you to make you help her like you should. Shame! Undt she nodt go to de school like you, undt learn better."

"I s'pose that's so," admitted Sadie, more thoughtfully. "She ain't a 'Merican like what I am, that goes to school an' learns from books."

In the end, between the ministrations of the Corner House girls and Mrs. Kranz, the whole Goronofsky family was made happy. Sadie promised to help her mamma without being bribed to do so; Mrs. Goronofsky, who was a worn, tired out little woman, proved to have some heart left for her step-daughter, after all; "the kids" were made delighted by the presents Sadie was enabled to bring them; and Ruth went around to Mr. Goronofsky's shop and presented him with a receipted bill for his house rent for December.

The work of the quartette of Lady Bountifuls by no means ended with the Goronofskys. Not a tenant of the Stower Estate was missed. Even Mrs. Kranz herself was remembered by the Corner House girls, who presented her, in combination, a handsome shopping bag to carry when she went downtown to the bank.

It was a busy afternoon and evening they spent on Meadow Street—for they did not get home to a late supper until eight o'clock. But their comments upon their adventures were characteristic.

"It is *so* satisfactory," said Ruth, placidly, "to make other people happy."

"I'm dog tired," declared Agnes, "but I'd love to start right out and do it all over again!"

"I—I hope the little Maroni baby won't lick all the red paint off that rattle and make herself sick," sighed Tess, reflectively.

"If she does we can buy her a new rattle. It didn't cost but ten cents," Dot rejoined, seeing at the moment but one side of the catastrophe.

CHAPTER XVII

"THAT CIRCUS BOY"

The first Christmas since the Kenway girls had "come into" Uncle Peter's estate was bound to be a memorable one for Ruth and Agnes and Tess and Dot.

Mother Kenway, while she had lived, had believed in the old-fashioned New England Christmas. The sisters had never had a tree, but they always hung their stockings on a line behind the "base-burner" in the sitting-room of the Bloomingsburg tenement. So now they hung them in a row by the dining-room mantelpiece in the old Corner House.

Uncle Rufus took a great deal of interest in this proceeding. He took out the fire-board from the old-fashioned chimney-place, so as to give ingress to Santa Clans when the reindeers of that good saint should land upon the Corner House roof.

Dot held to her first belief in the personal existence of Saint Nick, and although Tess had some doubts as to his real identity, she would not for the world have said anything to weaken Dot's belief.

There was no stove in the way in the dining-room, for the furnace—put into the cellar by Uncle Peter only shortly before his death—heated the two lower floors of the main part of the house, as well as the kitchen wing, in which the girls and Mrs. MacCall slept.

The girls had begged Neale O'Neil to hang up his stocking with theirs, but he refused—rather gruffly, it must be confessed. Mrs. MacCall and Uncle Rufus, however, were prevailed upon to add their hose to the line. Aunt Sarah rather snappishly objected to "exposing her stockings to the public view, whether on or off the person,"—so she said.

The four Corner House girls felt thankful to the queer old woman, who was really no relation to them at all, but who accepted all their bounty and attentions as though they were hers by right.

Indeed, at the time when there seemed some doubt as to whether Mr. Howbridge could prove for the Kenway girls a clear title to Uncle Peter's property, Aunt Sarah had furnished the necessary evidence, and sent away the claimant from Ipsilanti.

There was, too, a soft side to Aunt Sarah's character; only, like the chestnutburr, one had to get inside her shell to find it. If one of the children was ill, Aunt Sarah was right there with the old fashioned remedies, and although some of her "yarb teas" might be nasty to take, they were efficacious.

Then, she was always knitting, or embroidering, something or other for the girls. Now that there was plenty of money in the family purse, she ordered materials just as she pleased, and knit jackets, shawls, mittens, and "wristlets."

She was a very grim lady and dressed very plainly; although she never said so, she liked to have the girls sit with her at their sewing. She took infinite pains to teach them to be good needle-women, as her mother had doubtless taught her.

So the chief present the girls bought this Christmas for Aunt Sarah was a handsome sewing table, its drawers well supplied with all manner of threads, silks, wools, and such like materials.

This the Kenway sisters had all "chipped in" to purchase, and the table was smuggled into the house and hidden away in one of the spare rooms, weeks before Christmas. The girls had purchased a new dress for Mrs. MacCall, and had furnished out Uncle Rufus from top to toe in a suit of black clothes, with a white vest, in which he could wait at table on state and date occasions, as well as wear to church on Sundays.

There were, of course, small individual presents from each girl to these family retainers, and to Aunt Sarah. The stockings bulged most delightfully in the dining-room when they trooped down to breakfast on Christmas morning.

Tess and Dot could scarcely eat, their eyes were so fixed upon the delightfully knobby bundles piled under each of their stockings on the hearth. Agnes declared Tess tried to drink her buckwheat cakes and eat her coffee, and that Dot was in danger of sticking her fork into her eye instead of into her mouth.

But the meal was ended at last and Uncle Rufus wheeled out Aunt Sarah's beautiful sewing table, with her other smaller presents upon it. Ruth told her how happy it made them all to give it to her. Aunt Sarah's keen eye lit up as she was shown all the interesting things about her new acquisition; but all the verbal comment she made was that she thought "you gals better be in better business than buying gewgaws for an old woman like me."

"Just the same, she is pleased as Punch," Mrs. MacCall whispered to Ruth. "Only, she doesn't like to show it."

The girls quickly came to their own presents. None of the articles they had bought for each other were of great value intrinsically; but they all showed love and thoughtfulness. Little things that each had at some time carelessly expressed a wish for, appeared from the stockings to delight and warm the heart of the recipient.

There was nobody, of course, to give the two older girls any very valuable gifts; but there was a pretty locket and chain for Ruth which she had seen in the jewelry-store window and expressed a fondness for, while the desire of Agnes' eyes was satisfied when she found a certain bracelet in the toe of her stocking.

Tess had a bewildering number of books and school paraphernalia, as well as additions to her dolls' parapher-nalia; but it was Dot who sat down breathlessly in the middle of the floor under a perfect avalanche of treasures, all connected with her "children's" comfort and her personal house-keeping arrangements.

It would have been almost sacrilege to have presented Dot with another doll; for the Alice-doll that had come the Christmas before and had only lately been graduated into short clothes, still held the largest place in the little girl's affections.

Battered by adversity as the Alice-doll was, Dot's heart could never have warmed toward another "child" as it did toward the unfortunate that "Double Trouble"—that angel-faced young one from Ipsilanti—had buried with the dried apples. But Dot's sisters had showered upon her every imaginable comfort and convenience for the use of a growing family of dolls, as well as particular presents to the Alice-doll herself.

"What's the matter, child?" asked Mrs. MacCall, seeing the expression on Dot's face as she sat among her possessions. "Don't they suit?"

"Mrs. MacCall," declared Dot, gravely, "I think I shall faint. My heart's just jumping. If gladness could kill anybody, I know I'd have to die to show how happy I am. And I know my Alice-doll will feel just as I do."

Uncle Rufus' daughter, Petunia Blossom, came after breakfast with several of her brood—and the laundry cart—to take away the good things that had been gathered for her and her family.

Petunia was "fast brack," as her father declared—an enormously fat, jetty-black negress, with a pretty face, and a superabundance of children. To enumerate the Blossom family, as Petunia had once done for Ruth's information, there were:

"Two married and moved away; two at work; twins twice makes eight; Alfredia; Jackson Montgomery Simms; Burne-Jones Whistler; the baby; and Louisa Annette."

Ruth and her sisters had purchased, or made, small and unimportant presents for Neale O'Neil. Neale had remembered each of them with gifts, all the work of his own hands; a wooden berry dish and ladle for Tess' doll's tea-table; a rustic armchair for the Alice-doll, for Dot; a neatly made pencil box for Agnes; and for Ruth a new umbrella handle, beautifully carved and polished, for Ruth had a favorite umbrella the handle of which she had broken that winter.

Neale was ingenious in more ways than one. He showed this

at school, too, on several occasions. It was just after the midwinter holidays that Mr. Marks, the grammar school principal, wished to raise the school flag on the roof flag-staff, and it was found that the halyard and block had been torn away by the wind.

The janitor was too old a man to make the repair and it looked as though a professional rigger must be sent for, when Neale volunteered.

Perhaps Mr. Marks knew something about the boy's prowess, for he did not hesitate to give his permission. Neale went up to the roof and mounted the staff with the halyard rove through the block, and hooked the latter in place with ease. It took but a few minutes; but half the school stood below and held its breath, watching the slim figure swinging so recklessly on the flag-staff.

His mates cheered him when he came down, for they had grown fond of Neale O'Neil. The Corner House girls too, were proud of him. But Trix Severn, who disliked Neale because he paid her no attention, hearing Agnes praising the boy's courage and skill, exclaimed in her sneering way:

"That circus boy! Why wouldn't he be able to do all sorts of tricks like that? It was what he was brought up to, no doubt."

"What do you mean by that, Trix Severn?" demanded Agnes, immediately accepting her enemy's challenge. "Neale is not a circus boy."

"Oh! he isn't?"

"No. He's never even *seen* a circus," the positive Agnes declared.

"He told you that, did he?" laughed Trix, airily.

"He said he had never been to see a circus in his life," Agnes repeated. "And Neale wouldn't lie."

"That's all you know about him, then," said Trix. "And I thought you Corner House girls were such friends with Neale O'Neil," and she walked off laughing again, refusing to explain her insinuations.

But the nickname of "circus boy" stuck to Neale O'Neil after that and he earnestly wished he had not volunteered to fix the flag rigging. *Why* it troubled him so, however, he did not explain to the Corner House girls.

CHAPTER XVIII

SNOWBOUND

Tess said, gloomily, as they gathered about the study table one evening not long after New Year's:

"I have to write a composition about George Washington. When was he born, Ruthie?" Ruth was busy and did not appear to hear. "Say! when *was* he born?" repeated the ten-year-old.

"Eighteen seventy-eight, I think, dear," said Agnes, with more kindness than confidence.

"Oh-o-o!" gasped Dot, who knew something about the "Father of His Country." "He was dead-ed long before *that*."

"Before when?" demanded Ruth, partly waking up to the situation.

"Eighteen seventy-eight," repeated Tess, wearily.

"Of course I meant seventeen seventy-eight," interposed Agnes.

"And at that you're a long way off," observed Neale, who

chanced to be at the Corner House that evening.

"Well! you know so much, Mr. Smartie!" cried Agnes. "Tell her yourself."

"I wouldn't have given her the date of George's birth, as being right in the middle of the Revolutionary War," exclaimed Neale, stalling for time to figure out the right date.

"No; and you are not telling her *any* year," said the wise Agnes.

"Children! don't scrap," murmured peace-loving Ruth, sinking into the background—and her own algebra—again.

"Well!" complained Tess. "I haven't found out when he was born *yet*."

"Never mind, honey," said Agnes. "Tell what he *did*. That's more important. Look up the date later."

"I know," said Dot, breaking in with more primary information. "He planted a cherry tree."

"Chopped it down, you mean," said Agnes.

"And he never told a lie," insisted Dot.

"I believe that is an exploded doctrine," chuckled Neale O'Neil.

"Well, how did they *know* he didn't tell a lie?" demanded Tess, the practical.

"They never caught him in one," said Neale, with brutal frankness. "There's a whole lot of folks honest like *that*."

"Goodness, Neale!" cried Ruth, waking up again at *that* heresy. "How pessimistic you are."

"Was—was George Washington one of those things?" queried Tess, liking the sound of the long word.

"What things?" asked Ruth.

"Pes-sa-pessamisty?"

"Pessimistic? No, dear," laughed Ruth. "He was an optimist— or he never would have espoused the American cause."

"He was first in war, first in peace, and first in the hearts of his coun-try-men," sing-songed Dot.

"Oh, yes! I can put that in," agreed Tess, abandoning both the hard words Ruth had used, and getting back to safe details. "And he married a lady named Mary, didn't he?"

"No; Martha," said Agnes.

"Well, I knew it was one or the other, for we studied about Mary and Martha in our Sunday school lesson last Sunday," Tess said, placidly. "Martha was troubled about many things."

"I should think she would have been," remarked Dot, reflectively, "for George Washington had to fight Indians, and Britishers, and Hessians (who wore blue coats and big hats) and cabals—"

"Hold on!" shouted Neale. "What under the sun is a 'cabal'? A beast, or a bug?"

"Why, my teacher told us about George Washington," cried

Dot, with importance, "only a little while ago. And she said they raised a cabal against him—"

"That means a conspiracy," put in Ruth, quietly. "How can you folks study when you all talk so much?"

"Well, Martha," began Tess, when Ruth interposed:

"Don't get your Marthas mixed, dear."

"That's right, Tess," said Agnes. "George Washington's wife was not the sister of Lazarus—that's sure!"

"Oh, Aggie! how slangy you are!" cried Ruth.

Neale had slipped out after last speaking. He came in all of a bustle, stamping the snow from his feet on the hall rug.

"It's begun, girls!" he cried.

"Ye-es," admitted Tess, gravely. "I know it's begun; but I don't see how I am *ever* going to finish it."

"Oh, dear me, Tess! Let that old composition go for to-night," begged Agnes. "Do you mean it has begun to snow, Neale?"

"Like a regular old blizzard," declared Neale.

"Is it snowing as hard as it did the night we came from Carrie Poole's party?" asked Ruth, interested.

"Just come out on the porch and see," advised the boy, and they all trooped out after him—even Tess putting down her pencil and following at the rear of the procession.

It must have been snowing ever since supper time, for the lower step was already covered, and the air was thick with great, fleecy flakes, which piled drifts rapidly about every object in the Corner House back yard.

A prolonged "Oh!" came from every one. The girls could not see the street fence. The end of the woodshed was the limit of their vision down the long yard. Two or three fruit trees loomed like drooping ghosts in the storm.

"Wonderful! wonderful!" cried Ruth.

"No school to-morrow," Agnes declared.

"Well, I shall be glad, for one thing," said the worried Tess. "I won't have to bother about that old composition until another day."

Agnes was closely investigating the condition of the snow. "See!" she said, "it packs beautifully. Let's make a snowman."

"Goody-good!" squealed Dot. "That'll be *fun*!"

"I—don't—know," said Ruth, slowly. "It's late now—"

"But there'll be no school, Ruthie," Tess teased.

"Come on!" said Neale. "We can make a dandy."

"Well! Let us put on our warm things—and tell Mrs. MacCall," Ruth said, willing to be persuaded to get out into the white drifts.

When the girls came out, wrapped to the eyes, Neale already had several huge snowballs rolled. They got right to work with him, and soon their shrill laughter and jolly badinage assured all the neighborhood that the Corner House girls were out for a good time.

Yet the heavily falling snow seemed to cut them off like a wall from every other habitation. They could not even see the Creamers' cottage—and that was the nearest house.

It was great fun for the girls and their boy friend. They built a famous snowman, with a bucket for a cap, lumps of coal for eyes and nose, and stuck into its mouth an old long-stemmed clay pipe belonging to Uncle Rufus.

He was a jaunty looking snowman for a little while; but although he was so tall that the top of his hat was level with the peak of the woodshed roof, before the Corner House girls went to bed he stood more than knee deep in the drifted snow.

Neale had to make the round of his furnaces. Fortunately they were all in the neighborhood, but he had a stiff fight to get through the storm to the cobbler's little cottage before midnight.

At that "witching hour," if any of the Corner House girls had been awake and had looked out of the window, they would have seen that the snowman was then buried to his waist!

When daylight should have appeared, snow was still falling. A wind had arisen, and on one side of the old Corner House the drift entirely masked the windows. At eight o'clock they ate breakfast by lamplight.

Uncle Rufus did not get downstairs early, as he usually did, and when Tess ran up to call him, she found the old man groaning in his bed, and unable to rise.

"I done got de mis'ry in my back, chile," he said, feebly. "Don' yo' worry 'bout me none; I'll be cropin' down erbout noon."

But Mrs. MacCall would not hear to his moving. There was a small cylinder stove in his room (it was in the cold wing of the house) and she carried up kindling and a pail of coal and made a fire for him. Then Tess and Dot carried up his hot breakfast on one of the best trays, with a nice white napkin laid over it.

"Glo-*ree*! Chillen, yo' mak' a 'ninvalid out o' Unc' Rufus, an' he nebber wanter git up out'n hes baid at all. I don't spec' w'ite folkses to wait on me han' an' foot disher way— naw'm!"

"You're going to be treated just like one of the family, Uncle Rufus," cheerfully cried Ruth, who had likewise climbed the stairs to see him.

But somebody must do the chores. The back porch was mainly cleared; but a great drift had heaped up before it— higher than Ruth's head. The way to the side gate was shut off unless they tunneled through this drift.

At the end of the porch, however, was the entrance to the woodshed, and at the other end of the shed was a second door that opened upon the arbor path. The trellised grapevine extended ten yards from this door.

Ruth and Agnes ventured to this end door of the shed, and opened the swinging window in it. There was plenty of soft, fluffy snow under the grape-arbor, but not more than knee deep.

Against the arbor, on the storm side, the drift had packed up to the very top of the structure—and it was packed hard; but the lattice on the side had broken the snowfall and the path under the arbor could easily be cleared.

"Then we can get to the henhouse, Ruthie," said Agnes.

"And Billy Bumps, too, sister! Don't forget Billy Bumps," begged Tess from the porch.

"We'll try it, anyway," said Ruth. "Here are all the shovels, and we ought to be able to do it."

"Boys would," proclaimed Agnes.

"Neale would do it," echoed Dot, who had come out upon the porch likewise.

"I declare! I wish Neale were here right now," Ruth said.

"'If wishes were horses, beggars could ride,'" quoted Agnes. "Come on, Ruthie! I guess it's up to us."

First they went back into the kitchen to put on the warmest things they had—boots to keep their feet dry, and sweaters under their school coats, with stockingnet caps drawn down over their ears.

"I not only wish we *had* a boy in the family," grumbled Agnes, "but I wish *I* were that boy. What cumbersome clothes girls have to wear!"

"What do you want to wear—overalls and a jumper?" demanded Ruth, tartly.

"Fine!" cried her reckless sister. "If the suffragettes would demand the right to wear male garments instead of to vote,

I'd be a suffragette in a minute!"

"Disgraceful!" murmured Ruth.

"What?" cried Agnes, grinning. "To be a suffragette? Nothing of the kind! Lots of nice ladies belong to the party, and *we* may yet."

They had already been to the front of the old Corner House. A huge drift filled the veranda; they could not see Main Street save from the upper windows. And the flakes were still floating steadily downward.

"We're really snowbound," said Agnes, in some awe. "Do you suppose we have enough to eat in the house, to stand a long siege?"

"If we haven't," said Mrs. MacCall, from the pantry, "I'll fry you some snowballs and make a pot of icicle soup."

CHAPTER XIX

THE ENCHANTED CASTLE

It was plain that the streets would not be cleared *that* day. If the girls were able to get to school by the following Monday they would be fortunate.

None of the four had missed a day since the schools had opened in September, and from Ruth down, they did not wish to be marked as absent on their reports. This blizzard that had seized Milton in its grasp, however, forced the Board of Education to announce in the *Post* that pupils of all grades would be excused until the streets were moderately passable.

"Poor people will suffer a good deal, I am afraid," Ruth said, on this very first forenoon of their being snowbound.

"Our folks on Meadow Street," agreed Agnes. "I hope Mrs. Kranz will be kind to them."

"But we oughtn't to expect Mrs. Kranz, or Joe Maroni, to give away their food and coal. Then *they'd* soon be poor, too," said the earnest Ruth. "I tell you what, Aggie!"

"Well—shoot!"

Ruth overlooked her sister's slang for once. "We should leave money with Mrs. Kranz to help our poor folk, when we can't get over there to see them so frequently."

"Goodness, Ruth!" grumbled Agnes. "We won't have any spending money left for ourselves if we get into this charity game any deeper."

"Aren't you ashamed?" cried Ruth.

Agnes only laughed. They both knew that Agnes did not mean all that she said.

Ruth was already attacking the loose, fluffy snow under the arbor, and Agnes seized a spade and followed her older sister. It did not take such a great effort to get to the end of the arbor; but beyond that a great mass of hard-packed snow confronted them. Ruth could barely see over it.

"Oh, dear me!" groaned Agnes. "We'll never be able to dig a path through *that*."

This looked to be true to the older girl, too; so she began thinking. But it was Dot, trying to peer around the bigger girls' elbows, who solved the problem.

"Oh, my! how nice it would be to have a ladder and climb up to the top of that snowbank," she cried. "Maybe we could go over to Mabel Creamer's, right over the fence and all, Tess!"

"Hurray!" shouted Agnes. "We can cut steps in the bank, Ruth. Dot has given us a good idea—hasn't she?"

"I believe she has," agreed the oldest Kenway.

Although the snow had floated down so softly at first (and

was now coming in feathery particles) during the height of the storm, the wind had blown and it had been so cold that the drifts were packed hard.

Without much difficulty the girls made four steps up out of the mouth of the grape-arbor, to the surface of the drift. Then they tramped a path on top to the door of the henhouse.

By this same entrance they could get to the goat's quarters. The snow had drifted completely over the henhouse, but that only helped to keep the hens and Billy Bumps warm.

Later the girls tunneled through the great drift at the back porch, leaving a thick arch which remained for the rest of the week. So they got a path broken to the gate on Willow Street.

The snowman had disappeared to his shoulders. It continued to snow most of that day and the grape-arbor path became a perfect tunnel.

There was no school until Monday. Even then the streets were almost impassable for vehicles. The Highway Department of the town was removing the drifts in the roads and some of this excavated snow was dumped at the end of the Parade Ground, opposite the schools.

The boys hailed these piles of snow as being fine for fortifications, and snowball battles that first day waxed furious.

Then the leading spirits among the boys—including Neale O'Neil—put their heads together and the erection of the enchanted castle was begun. But more of *that* anon.

Tess had had plenty of time to write that composition on the

"Father of His Country." Indeed, Miss Andrews should have had a collection of wonderfully good biographical papers handed in by her class on that Monday morning.

But Tess's was not all that might be desired as a sketch of George Washington's life, and the teacher told her so. Still, she did better with her subject than Sadie Goronofsky did with hers.

Sadie had been given Longfellow to write about, and Miss Andrews showed the composition to Agnes' teacher as an example of what could be done in the line of disseminating *mis*information about the Dead and the Great. Miss Shipman allowed Agnes to read it.

"Longfellow was a grand man; he wrote both poems and poetry. He graduated at Bowdoin and afterward taught in the same school where he graduated. He didn't like teaching and decided to learn some other trade, so his school furnished him money to go to Europe and learn to be a poet. After that he wrote many beautiful rhymes for children. He wrote 'Billy, the Blacksmith,' and Hiwater, what I seen in a pitcher show."

"Well, Sadie maybe doesn't know much about poets," said Tess, reflectively, when she heard her older sisters laughing about the funny composition. "But she knows numbers, and can multiply and divide. But then, Maria Maroni can make change at her father's stand, and she told Miss Andrews of all the holidays, she liked most the Fourth of July, because that was when America was discovered. Of course *that* isn't so," concluded Tess.

"When was it discovered?" asked Ruth.

"Oh, I know! I know!" cried Dot, perilously balancing a

spoonful of mush and milk on the way to her mouth, in midair. "It was in 1492 at Thanksgiving time, and the Pilgrim Fathers found it first. So they called it Plymouth Rock—and you've got some of their hens in your hen-yard, Ruthie."

"My goodness!" gasped Agnes, after she had laughed herself almost out of her chair over this. "These primary minds are like sieves, aren't they? All the information goes through, while the mis-information sticks."

"Huh!" said Tess, vexed for the moment. "You needn't say anything, Aggie. You told us George Washington was born in 1778 and teacher gave me a black mark on *that*."

As that week progressed and the cold weather continued, a really wonderful structure was raised on the Parade Ground opposite the main door of the Milton High School. The boys called it the snow castle and a reporter for the *Post* wrote a piece about it even before it was finished.

Boys of all grades, from the primary up, had their "fingers in the pie"; for the very youngest could roll big snowballs on the smooth lawns of the Parade at noon when the sun was warm, and draw them to the site of the castle on their sleds after school was over for the day.

The bigger boys built up the walls, set in the round windows of ice, which were frozen each night in washtubs and brought carefully to the castle. The doorway was a huge arch, with a sheet of ice set in at the top like a fanlight over an old-fashioned front door. A flat roof was made of planks, with snow shoveled upon them and tramped down.

Several pillars of fence rails were set up inside to keep the roof from sagging; then the castle was swept out, the floor smoothed, and the girls were allowed to enter.

It was a fine, big snowhouse, all of forty feet long and half as wide. It was as large as a small moving picture place.

Somebody suggested having moving pictures in it—or a magic lantern show, but Joe Eldred, one of the bigger high school boys, whose father was superintendent of the Milton Electric Lighting Company, had a better idea than that.

On Thursday, when the castle was all finished, and the *Post* had spoken of it, Joe went to his father and begged some wire and rigging, and the boys chipped in to buy several sixty-watt lamps.

Joe Eldred was a young electrician himself, and Neale O'Neil aided him, for Neale seemed to know a lot about electric lighting. When his mates called him "the circus boy," Neale scowled and said nothing, but he was too good-natured and polite to refuse to help in any general plan for fun like this now under way.

Joe got a permit from Mr. Eldred and then they connected up the lamps they had strung inside the castle and at the entrance, with the city lighting cables.

At dusk that Thursday evening, the snowhouse suddenly burst into illumination. The sheets of clear ice made good windows. Christmas greens were festooned over the entrance, and around the walls within.

After supper the boys and girls gathered in and about the snow castle; somebody brought a talking machine from home and played some dance records. The older girls, and some of the boys, danced.

But the castle was not ornate enough to suit the builders. The next day they ran up a false-front with a tower at either side. These towers were partly walled with ice, too, and the boys illuminated them that night.

Saturday the boys were busier than ever, and they spread broadcast the announcement of a regular "ice-carnival" for that evening.

After the crowd had gone away on Friday night, a few of the boys remained and flooded the floor of the castle. This floor was now smoothly frozen, and the best skaters were invited to come Saturday night and "show off."

By evening, too, the battlements of the castle had been raised on all four sides. At each corner was a lighted tower, and in the middle of the roof a taller pinnacle had been raised with a red, white, and blue star, in colored electric bulbs, surmounting it.

Milton had never seen such an exhibition before, and a crowd turned out—many more people than could possibly get into the place at once. There was music, and the skating was attractive. Visitors were allowed in the castle, but they were obliged to keep moving, having to walk down one side of the castle, and up the other, so as to give those behind a chance to see everything.

The Corner House girls had thought the enchanted castle (for so it looked to be from their windows at home) a very delightful object. Ruth and Agnes went up after supper on Saturday evening, with their skates.

Both of them were good skaters and Neale chose Aggie to skate with him in the carnival. Joe Eldred was glad to get Ruth. Carrie and Lucy Poole were paired off with two of the big boys, and *they* were nowhere near as good skaters as Trix Severn.

Yet Trix was neglected. She had to go alone upon the ice, or skate with another girl. There was a reason for this neglect that Trix could not appreciate. Boys do not like to escort a girl who is always "knocking" some other girl. The boys declared Trix Severn "carried her hammer" wherever she went and they steered clear of her when they wanted to have a good time.

Every time Agnes and Neale O'Neil passed Trix Severn upon the ice, she was made almost ill with envy!

CHAPTER XX

TRIX SEVERN IN PERIL

That cold spell in January was a long one. The young folk of Milton had plenty of sledding, and some skating. But the snow-ice on Milton Pond was "hubbly" and not nice to skate on, while there were only a few patches of smooth ice anywhere in town.

Therefore the boys never failed to flood the interior of the snow castle each night before they went home. They did this easily by means of a short piece of fire-hose attached to the nearby hydrant.

Taking pattern of this idea, Neale O 'Neil made a small pond for the two youngest Corner House girls in the big garden at the rear of the house. Here Tess could practise skating to her heart's content, and even Dot essayed the art.

But the latter liked better to be drawn about on her sled, with the Alice-doll in her arms, or perhaps one of the cats.

Bungle, Dot's own particular pet among Sandyface's children, was now a great lazy cat; but he was gentle. Dorothy could do anything with him—and with Popocatepetl, as well.

One day the doctor's wife came to call at the old Corner House. The doctor and his wife were a childless couple and that was why, perhaps, they both had developed such a deep interest in the four girls who made the old Stower homestead so bright and lively.

Dr. Forsyth never met Dot on the street with the Alice-doll without stopping to ask particularly after the latter's health. He said he felt himself to be consultant in general and family physician for all Dot's brood of doll-babies, for the Kenway sisters were far too healthy to need his attention in any degree.

"If all my customers were like you girls," he declared, in his jovial way, "I'd have to take my pills and powders to another shop."

Ruth knew that Mr. Howbridge had insisted at first that Dr. Forsyth "look over" the Corner House girls, once in so often. But just for himself, she was always glad to see the doctor's ruddy, smiling face approaching. The girls were all fond of Mrs. Forsyth, too, for she did not come professionally. On the occasion referred to, Mrs. Forsyth was ushered by Mrs. MacCall, quite unexpectedly, into the back parlor, or sitting-room, which the family used a good deal nowadays.

The lady had been out for an airing in the doctor's two-seated sleigh and she brought in with her a cunning little Pomeranian dog of which she was very fond.

It was a pretty, harmless little beast and the Corner House girls thought Tootsie awfully cunning. Other members of the household did not look upon the Pomeranian, however, in the same light.

Dot was apparently the single occupant of the sitting-room

when Mrs. Forsyth bustled in. "I'll tell the girls," Mrs. MacCall said, briskly, and she shut the visitor into the room, for on this cold day the big front hall was draughty.

Mrs. Forsyth put the Pomeranian down at once and advanced toward the register. "Well, my dear!" she cried, seeing Dot. "How do you do, child? Come give Auntie Forsyth a kiss. I declare! I get hungry for little girl's kisses, so few of them come my way."

"Goodness! what have you there?"

For what she had supposed to be two gaily dressed dolls sitting side by side upon the sofa behind Dot, had suddenly moved. Mrs. Forsyth was a little near-sighted, anyway, and now she was without her glasses, while her eyes were watering because of the cold.

"Why," said Dot, in a most matter-of-fact way, "it's only Bungle and Popocatepetl."

"Popo—*who*?" gasped Mrs. Forsyth, at that amazing name.

Dot repeated it. She had learned to pronounce it perfectly and was rather proud of the accomplishment.

There was another movement on the sofa. The two cats were dressed in doll clothes, and their activities were somewhat restricted, but they had sensed the presence of the dog the instant it had come into the room.

"Oh! oh!" cried Dot, suddenly. "Bungle! you be good. Petal! don't you dare move!"

The cheerful little dog, quite unsuspicious of harm, had trotted after its mistress. Despite the clinging doll clothes, the tails of Bungle and Popocatepetl swelled, their backs went up, and they began to spit!

"Tootsie!" screamed the doctor's wife in alarm.

Dot shouted at the cats, too, but neither they, nor the dog, were in a mood to obey. The Pomeranian was too scared, and Bungle and Popocatepetl were too angry.

Tootsie saw her enemies just as the cats leaped. Hampered by the garments Dot had put upon them, both Bungle and Popocatepetl went head-over-heels when they first landed on the floor, and with a frightened "ki, yi!" Tootsie distanced them to the far end of the room.

There was no cover there for the terrified pup, and when the two cats—clawing at the dresses and threatening vengeance—came after the dog, Tootsie tried to crawl under the three-sided walnut "whatnot" that stood in the corner between the windows.

The whatnot was shaky, having only three short, spindle legs. Tootsie darted under and then darted out again. Bungle got in one free-handed slap at the little dog as she went under, while Popocatepetl caught her on the rebound as Tootsie came out.

The long, silky hair of the dog saved her from any injury. But she was so scared that she yelped as though the claws of both cats had torn her.

"Oh! my poor Tootsie!" wailed the doctor's wife. "They will kill her."

Dot stood, open mouthed. She could not quench the fury of the angered cats.

"That—that's my Alice-doll's next-to-best dress, Bungle!" she managed to say. "You're tearing it! you're tearing it!"

Just then the door opened. Uncle Rufus came tottering in with the feather duster. The old man's rheumatism still troubled him and he was not steady on his feet.

Tootsie saw a way of escape. She darted between Uncle Rufus' legs, still yelping as loudly as she could.

"Wha' fo' dat? wha' fo' dat?" ejaculated Uncle Rufus, and he fell back against the door which closed with a slam. If Tootsie had possessed a long tail it certainly would have been caught.

"Git erway f'om yere, you pesky cats!" shouted Uncle Rufus as Bungle and Popocatepetl charged the door on the trail of the terrified dog.

"Oh, dear me! Don't let them out," begged Dot, "till I can get my doll's clothes off."

"My poor Tootsie!" cried Mrs. Forsyth again.

"Hush yo'! hush yo'!" said Uncle Rufus, kindly. "Dar's a do' shet 'twixt dat leetle fice an' dem crazy cats. Dar's sho' nuff wot de papahs calls er armerstice 'twixt de berlig'rant pahties—ya-as'm! De berry wust has happen' already, so yo' folkses might's well git ca'm—git ca'm."

The old colored man's philosophy delighted the doctor's wife so much that she had to laugh. Yet she was not wholly assured that Tootsie was not hurt until the older girls had trailed the Pomeranian under the bed in one of the chambers. She had only been hurt in her feelings.

The cats could not seem to calm down either, and Uncle Rufus had to hold one after the other while Dot removed what remained of the doll's clothes, in which she had decked out her favorites.

"I guess I don't want cats for doll-babies any more," Dot said, with gravity, examining a scratch on her plump wrist, after supper that evening. "They don't seem able to learn the business—not *good*."

Agnes laughed, and sing-songed:

"Cats delight
To scratch and bite,
For 'tis their nature to;
But pretty dolls
With curly polls,
Have something else to do."

"I think our Aggie is going to be a poetess," said Tess, to Ruth, secretly. "She rhymes so easy!"

"I'd rather have her learn to pick up her things and put them properly away," said Ruth, who was trying to find her own out-door clothing on the back hall rack. "My goodness! everything I put my hand on belongs to Agnes."

"That's because I'm rich," returned Agnes cheerfully. "For once in my life I have a multitude of clothes," and she started off, cheerfully whistling and swinging her skates. Ruth had almost to run to catch up with her before she struck across into the Parade.

The weather had moderated that day, and at noon the gutters were flooded and the paths ran full streams. The boys, however, had pronounced the ice in the snow castle to be in fine shape.

"Perhaps this will be the last night we can skate there," Ruth said as they tramped along the Parade walk, side by side.

"Oh, I hope not!" cried Agnes.

"But Neale says the weight of the towers and the roof of the castle will maybe make the walls slump right down there, if it begins to thaw."

"Oh! I don't believe it," said Agnes, who did not *want* to believe it. "It looks just as strong!"

They could see the gaily illuminated snow castle through the branches of the leafless trees. The fiery star above it and the lights below shining through the ice-windows, made it very brilliant indeed.

"Well," Ruth said, with a sigh, "if the boys say it isn't safe, we mustn't go in to-night, Agnes."

There were only a few young folk already assembled about the castle when the Corner House girls arrived. A man in a blue uniform with silver buttons, had just come out of the castle with Joe Eldred and Neale O'Neil.

"I don't know whether it's safe, or not," the fireman was saying. "Give me a frame building, and I can tell all right and proper. But I never ran to a fire in a snowhouse, and I don't know much about them—that's a fact," and he laughed.

Neale looked serious when he walked over to the two Corner House girls.

"What's the matter, Sir Lachrymose?" demanded Agnes, gaily.

"I believe the further wall of this snowhouse has slumped," he said. "Maybe there is no danger, but I don't know."

"Oh, nobody will go in, of course," Ruth cried.

"Sure they will, Ruth. Don't be a goose," said Agnes, sharply.

"*I* certainly will not," her sister said. "It was real warm this noon and maybe the house is just tottering. Isn't that so, Neale?"

"I don't know," said the boy. "Wish I did."

"Let's go in and find out," said Agnes, the reckless.

"Wait," drawled Neale. "I'd rather find out, out here than in there—especially if the thing is coming down."

"There goes Trix Severn—and Wilbur Ketchell," said Agnes, rather crossly. "They're going to risk it."

"Let them go, Aggie," said Neale. "I'm not going into that place until I'm sure."

"Nor am I," Ruth announced, with emphasis.

"Well, I don't see—" Agnes began, when Neale exclaimed:

"Wait. Joe's stopped them."

Eldred had interfered when Trix and her escort started into the snow castle. The Corner House girls and Neale drew near.

"I don't care!" Trix was saying in her loud voice. "I'm going to skate. Oh! don't bother to tell me it isn't safe, Joe Eldred. You just want to keep me off the ice."

She was already sitting on a rough bench that had been drawn there by the boys, and Wilbur was putting on her skates.

"You always do know it all, Trix," Joe said, sharply, "but I advise you to go slow—"

The obstinate girl stood up as Wilbur finished with the last strap. She laughed in Joe's face.

"You make me tired, Joe Eldred," she observed, and without waiting for further parley she shot away into the otherwise empty castle.

"Oh! why didn't you stop her?" cried Ruth, anxiously.

"I'd like to see anybody stop *that* girl," growled Joe.

"She's as reckless as she can be," said Neale.

"Aw, say!" exclaimed Wib, as they called young Ketchell, "is the roof really unsafe?"

"We don't know," Neale said, in a worried tone. Then suddenly there was a sharp crack from inside the snow castle.

"Crickey! it's coming down!" exclaimed Wilbur.

"What *was* that, Neale?" demanded Joe Eldred.

"That pillar's gone!" exclaimed Neale O'Neil, pointing to one of the wooden supports by which the roof of planks and snow was partly upheld.

On the tail of his declaration there was another crash and a second support, farther down the hall, was splintered.

"The roof's coming down, Trix! Come back! come back!" shrieked Agnes.

Trix was at the far end. She had turned swiftly and they could see her face. The wooden supports giving way between her and the exit frightened the reckless girl immeasurably.

"Come back, Trix!" Ruth added her cry to her sister's.

The electric lights began to quiver. The whole mass of the roof must be sagging down. Ketchell kicked off his skates and picked them up, preparatory to getting out of the way.

And perhaps it was just as well that he had showed no heroism. Had he skated in for the girl, he could not have aided her in any way.

Trix started for the front of the snow castle. They saw her stoop forward and put on speed, and then—in a flash—the middle of the roof settled and crashed to the floor—and the sound of the wreck almost deafened the onlookers!

CHAPTER XXI

A BACKYARD CIRCUS

They said afterward that the wreck of the snow castle was heard clear to the outskirts of the town. The *Morning Post* said that it was disgraceful that the school authorities had allowed it to be built. Parents and guardians were inclined to rail against what they had previously praised the boys for doing.

The fact remained, and the calmer people of the community admitted it, that as soon as there was any danger the boys had warned everybody out. That one headstrong girl—and she, only—was caught in the wreckage, did not change the fact that the boys had been very careful.

At the moment the roof of the snow castle crashed in, the only thought of those in sight of the catastrophe was of Trix Severn.

"Oh! save her! save her!" Ruth Kenway cried.

"She's killed! I *know* she is!" wept Agnes, wringing her hands.

Joe Eldred and Wib Ketchell were as pale as they could be.

None of the little group at the entrance moved for a full minute. Then Neale O'Neil brought them all to life with:

"*She wasn't under that fall!* Quick! 'round to the rear! We can save her."

"I tell you she's dead!" avowed Wilbur, hoarsely.

"Come on!" shouted Neale, and seized a shovel that stood leaning against the snow wall. "Come on, Joe! The roof's only fallen in the middle. Trix is back of that, I tell you!"

"Neale is right! Neale is right!" screamed Agnes. "Let's dig her out."

She and Ruth started after Neale O'Neil and Joe. Wilbur ran away in terror and did much to spread the senseless alarm throughout the neighborhood that half the school children in town were buried beneath the wreckage of the snow castle!

But it was bad enough—at first. The Corner House girls and their boy friends were not altogether sure that Trix was only barred from escape by the falling rubbish.

Neale and Joe attacked the rear wall of the structure with vigor, but the edge of their shovels was almost turned by the icy mass. Axes and crowbars would scarcely have made an impression on the hard-packed snow.

It was Ruth who pointed the right way. She picked up a hard lump of snow and sent it crashing through the rear ice-window!

"Trix!" she shouted.

"Oh! get me out! get me out!" the voice of the missing

girl replied.

Another huge section of the roof, with the side battlements, caved inward; but it was a forward section.

The boys knocked out the rest of the broken ice around the window-hole and Neale leaped upon the sill which was more than three feet across. The walls of the castle were toppling, and falling, and the lights had gone out. But there was a moon and the boy could see what he was about.

The spectators at a distance were helpless during the few minutes which had elapsed since the first alarm. Nobody came to the assistance of the Corner House girls and the two boys.

But Trix was able to help herself. Neale saw her hands extended, and he leaned over and seized her wrists, while Joe held him by the feet.

Then with a heave, and wriggle, "that circus boy," as Trix had nicknamed him, performed the feat of getting her out of the falling castle, and the Corner House girls received her with open arms.

The peril was over, but rumor fed the excitement for an hour and brought out as big a crowd as though there had been a fire in the business section of the town.

Trix clung to Ruth and Agnes Kenway in an abandonment of terror and thanksgiving, at first. The peril she had suffered quite broke down her haughtiness, and the rancor she had felt toward the Corner House girls was dissipated.

"There, there! Don't you cry any more, Trix," urged good-natured Agnes. "I'm *so* glad you got out of that horrid place safely. And we didn't help you, you know. It was Neale O'Neil."

"That circus boy" had slunk away as though he had done something criminal; but Joe was blowing a horn of praise for Neale in the crowd, as the Corner House girls led Trix away.

Ruth and Agnes went home with Trix Severn, but they would not go into the house that evening as Trix desired. The very next morning Trix was around before schooltime, to walk to school with Agnes. And within a week (as Neale laughingly declared to Ruth) Agnes and Trix were "as thick as thieves!"

"Can you beat Aggie?" scoffed Neale. "That Trix girl has been treating her as mean as she knows how for months, and now you couldn't pry Aggie away from her with a crowbar."

"I am glad," said Ruth, "that Agnes so soon gets over being mad."

"Huh! Trix is soft just now. But wait till she gets mad again," he prophesied.

However, this intimacy of Agnes with her former enemy continued so long that winter passed, and spring tiptoed through the woods and fields, flinging her bounties with lavish hand, while still Agnes and Trix remained the best of friends.

As spring advanced, the usual restless spirit of the season pervaded the old Corner House. Especially did the little girls find it infectious. Tess and Dot neglected the nursery and the dolls for the sake of being out-of-doors.

Old Billy Bumps, who had lived almost the life of a hermit

for part of the winter, was now allowed the freedom of the premises for a part of each day. They kept the gates shut; but the goat had too good a home, and led too much a life of ease here at the Corner House, to wish to wander far.

The girls ran out to the rescue of any stranger who came to the Willow Street gate. It was not everybody that Billy Bumps "took to," but many he "took after."

When he took it into his hard old head to bump one, he certainly bumped hard—as witness Mr. Con Murphy's pig that he had butted through the fence on the second day of his arrival at the old Corner House.

That particular pig had been killed, but there was another young porker now in the cobbler's sty. Neale O'Neil continued to lodge with Mr. Con Murphy. He was of considerable help to the cobbler, and the little Irishman was undoubtedly fond of the strange boy.

For Neale *did* remain a stranger, even to his cobbler friend, as Mr. Murphy told Ruth and Agnes, when they called on him on one occasion.

"An oyster is a garrulous bir-r-rd beside that same Neale O'Neil. I know as much about his past now as I did whin he kem to me—which same is jist nawthin' at all, at all!"

"I don't believe he *has* a past!" cried Agnes, eager to defend her hero.

"Sure, d'ye think the bye is a miracle?" demanded Con Murphy. "That he has no beginning and no ending? Never fear! He has enough to tell us if he would, and some day the dam of his speech will go busted, and we'll hear it all."

"Is he afraid to tell us who he really is?" asked Ruth, doubtfully.

"I think so, Miss," said the cobbler. "He is fearin' something—that I know. But phat that same is, I dunno!"

Neale O'Neil had made good at school. He had gained the respect of Mr. Marks and of course Miss Georgiana liked him. With the boys and girls of grade six, grammar, he was very popular, and he seemed destined to graduate into high school in June with flying colors.

June was still a long way off when, one day, Tess and Dot begged Neale to harness Billy Bumps to the wagon for them. Uncle Rufus had fashioned a strong harness and the wagon to which the old goat was attached had two seats. He was a sturdy animal and had been well broken; so, if he wished to do so, he could trot all around the big yard with Tess and Dot in the cart.

Sometimes Billy Bumps did not care to play pony; then it was quite impossible to do anything with him. But he was never rough with, or offered to butt, Tess and Dot. They could manage his goatship when nobody else could.

Sometimes Billy Bumps' old master, Sammy Pinkney, came over to see his former pet, but the bulldog, Jock, remained outside the gate. Billy Bumps did not like Jock, and he was never slow to show his antagonism toward the dog.

On this occasion that Neale harnessed the goat to the wagon, there was no trouble at first. Billy Bumps was feeling well and not too lazy. Tess and Dot got aboard, and the mistress of the goat seized the reins and clucked to him.

Billy Bumps drove just like a pony—and was quite as well

trained. The little girls guided him all around the garden, and then around the house, following the bricked path down to the front gate.

They never went outside with Billy unless either Neale, or Uncle Rufus, was with them, for there was still a well developed doubt in the minds of the older folk as to what Billy Bumps might do if he took it into his head to have a "tantrum."

"As though our dear old Billy Bumps would do anything naughty!" Dot said. "But, as you say, Tess, we can't go out on Main Street with him unless we ask."

"And Uncle Rufus is busy," said Tess, turning the goat around.

They drove placidly around the house again to the rear, following the path along the Willow Street side.

"There's Sammy Pinkney," said Dot.

"Well, I hope he doesn't come in," said Tess, busy with the reins. "He is too rough with Billy Bumps."

But Sammy came in whistling, with his cap very far back on his closely cropped head, and the usual mischievous grin on his face. Jock was at his heels and Billy Bumps immediately stopped and shook his head.

"Now, you send that dog right back, Sammy," commanded Tess. "You know Billy Bumps doesn't like him."

"Aw, I didn't know Jock was following me," explained Sammy, and he drove the bulldog out of the yard. But he failed to latch the gate, and Jock was too faithful to go far away.

Billy Bumps was still stamping his feet and shaking his head. Sam came up and began to rub his ears—an attention for which the goat did not care.

"Don't tease him, Sammy," begged Dot.

"Aw, I'm not," declared Sammy.

"He doesn't like that—you know he doesn't," admonished Tess.

"He ought to have gotten used to it by this time," Sammy declared. "Jinks! what's that?"

Unnoticed by the children, Sandyface, the old mother cat, had gravely walked down the path to the street gate. She was quite oblivious of the presence, just outside, of Jock, who crouched with the very tip of his red tongue poked out and looking just as amiable as it is ever possible for a bulldog to look.

Suddenly Jock spied Sandyface. The dog was instantly all attention—quivering muzzle, twitching ears, sides heaving, even his abbreviated tail vibrating with delighted antici- pation. Jock considered cats his rightful prey, and Sammy was not the master to teach him better.

The dog sprang for the gate, and it swung open. Sandyface saw her enemy while he was in midair.

She flew across the backyard to the big pear-tree. Jock was right behind her, his tongue lolling out and the joy of the chase strongly exhibited in his speaking countenance.

In his usual foolish fashion, the bulldog tried to climb the tree after the cat. Jock could never seem to learn that he was not fitted by nature for such exploits, and wherever the game led, he tried to follow.

His interest being so completely centered in Sandyface and his attempt to get her, peril in the rear never crossed Jock's doggish mind.

Old Billy Bumps uttered a challenging "blat" almost upon the tail of Sammy's shout; then he started headlong for his ancient enemy. He gave his lady passengers no time to disembark, but charged across the yard, head down, and aimed directly at the leaping bulldog.

The latter, quite unconscious of impending peril, continued to try to catch Sandyface, who looked down upon his foolish gyrations from a branch near the top of the tree. Perhaps she divined what was about to happen to the naughty Jock, for she did not even meow!

CHAPTER XXII

MR. SORBER

Tess had presence of mind enough to holloa "Whoa!" and she kept right on saying it. Usually it was effective, but on this occasion Billy Bumps was deaf to his little mistress.

Dot clung to Tess's shoulders and screamed. There was really nothing else for her to do.

Sammy had grabbed at the goat's horns and was promptly overthrown. They left him roaring on his back upon the brick walk, while the goat tore on, dragging the bumping wagon behind him.

Billy Bumps had not earned his name without reason. Having taken aim at the bulldog jumping up and down against the trunk of the pear tree, nothing but a solid wall could have stopped him.

There was a crash as one forward wheel of the cart went over a stone. Out toppled Tess and Dot upon the soft earth.

Billy Bumps went on and collided with Jock, much to that animal's surprise and pain. The bulldog uttered a single yelp as the goat got him between his hard horns and the treetrunk.

Grace Brooks Hill

"You stop that, Billy!" roared Sam, struggling to his feet. "Let my dog alone."

But Jock was not likely to give the goat a second chance. He limped away, growling and showing his teeth, while Billy Bumps tried to free himself of the harness so as to give pursuit.

"Don't you hurt Billy!" Tess screamed at Sam, getting to her feet and helping Dot to rise.

"I'd like to knock him!" cried Sam.

"You ought to keep your dog out of our yard!" declared Tess. Dot was crying a little and the older girl was really angry.

"I'll set him onto that Billy Bumps next time I get a chance," growled Sam.

"You dare!" cried Tess.

But Jock was already outside of the yard. When Sam whistled for him, he only wagged his stump of a tail; he refused to return to a place where, it was plain to his doggish intelligence, he was not wanted. Besides, Jock had not yet gotten a full breath since the goat butted him.

Sammy picked up a clothes-pole and started to punish Billy Bumps as he thought fit. Just then the goat got free from the cart and started for Master Pinkney. The latter dropped the pole and got to the gate first, but only just in time, for Billy crashed head-first into it, breaking a picket, he was so emphatic!

"You wait! I'll kill your old goat," threatened Sammy, shaking his fist over the fence. "You see if I don't, Tess

Kenway," forgetting, it seemed, that it had been he who had presented the goat to the Corner House girl.

Billy trotted back proudly to the girls to be petted, as though he had done a very meritorious act. Perhaps he had, for Sandyface at once came down from the tree, to sit on the porch in the sunshine and "wash her face and hands"; she doubtless considered Billy Bumps very chivalrous.

The great hullabaloo brought most of the family to the scene, as well as Neale from over the back fence. But the fun was all over and Sammy and his bulldog were gone when the questioners arrived.

Dot explained volubly: "Billy Bumps wouldn't see poor Sandy abused—no, he wouldn't! That's why he went for that horrid dog."

"Why," said Ruth, laughing, "Billy must be a regular knight."

"'In days of old, when knights were bold!'" sang Neale.

"I've an improvement on *that*," Agnes said, eagerly. "Listen:

"'Sir Guy, a knight,
In armor bright,
Took tea with Mistress Powsers.
With manner free,
She spilled the tea,
And rusted Guy's best trousers!'"

"Then he certainly must have looked *a guy*!" Neale declared. "I always wondered how those 'knights of old' got along in their tin uniforms. After a campaign in wet weather they must have been a pretty rusty looking bunch."

It was about this time that Neale O'Neil got his name in the local paper, and the Corner House girls were very proud of him.

Although Neale was so close-mouthed about his life before his arrival in Milton, the girls knew he was fond of, and had been used to, horses. If he obtained a job on Saturday helping a teamster, or driving a private carriage, he enjoyed *that* day's work, if no other.

On a certain Saturday the girls saw Neale drive by early in the morning with a handsome pair of young horses, drawing loam to a part of the Parade ground which was to be re-seeded. The contractor had only recently bought these young horses from the West, but he trusted Neale with them, for he knew the boy was careful and seemed able to handle almost any kind of a team.

The Kenway sisters went shopping that afternoon as usual. The end of Main Street near Blachstein and Mapes depart-ment store, and the Unique Candy Store, and other shops that the sisters patronized, were filled with shoppers. Milton was a busy town on Saturdays.

Tess and Dot were crossing the street at Ralph Avenue when a shouting up Main Street made them turn to look that way. People in the street scattered and certain vehicles were hastily driven out of the way of a pair of horses that came charging down the middle of Main Street like mad.

Ruth saw the danger of her younger sisters, and called to them from the doorway of the drugstore.

"Tess! Dot! Quick! Come here!"

But Agnes ran from across the street and hustled the smaller girls upon the sidewalk. Then they could all give their attention to the runaway.

Not until then did they realize that it was the team Neale O'Neil had been driving. An auto horn had startled them at the Parade Ground, while Neale was out of the wagon, and downtown they started.

It seemed to the onlookers as though the team traveled faster every block! Nevertheless Neale had chased and overtaken the wagon not far below the old Corner House.

He clambered over the tailboard and, as the wagon rocked from side to side and its noise spurred the maddened horses to greater speed, the boy plunged forward and climbed into the seat.

The reins had been torn from the whipstock; they were dragging in the street. It looked for the moment as though Neale had risked his life for nothing. He could not halt the runaways!

Another boy might have failed, even after getting that far; but not "that circus boy"!

People along the street set up a shout when they beheld Neale O'Neil leap right down on the pole of the wagon and stretch out perilously to seize the reins at the hames. He had them and was back in the seat before the horses had run another block.

As he passed Ralph Avenue where the Corner House girls stood, he had lost his hat; his hair, which had grown long again, was blowing back in the wind, and his white face was a mask of determination.

"Oh! he'll be killed!" whispered Ruth.

"He's going to stop them!" crowed Agnes, with assurance.

And so Neale did. He stopped them as soon as he could get into the seat, brace his feet, and obtain a purchase on the lines. He knew how to break the horses' hold on the bits, and sawing at their mouths sharply, he soon brought them to a stop.

He tried to drive back to his work then without being accosted by the crowd that quickly gathered. But the reporter from the *Post* was right on the spot and the next morning a long article appeared on the front page of the paper about the runaway and about the youngster who had played the hero.

Because Neale refused to talk to the reporter himself, other people had talked for him, and quite a little romance about Neale was woven into the story. Even the fact that he went by the nickname of "the circus boy" at school got into the story, and it was likewise told how he had made a high mark in gymnastics.

Neale seemed terribly cut-up when the girls showed him the article in the paper. "Why," said Ruth, "you ought to be proud."

"Of that tattling business?" snapped Neale.

"No. Not so much that the paper speaks well of you, but because of your ability to do such a thing," said the oldest Corner House girl. "It isn't every boy that could do it."

"I should hope not!" growled Neale, emphatically. "Let me tell you," he added, angrily, "the reason I can do such things is the reason why I am such an ignorant fellow—and so far behind other chaps of my age."

And that is the nearest Neale had ever come to saying anything directly about his old life. That it had been hard, and unpleasant, and that he had been denied the benefits of schooling were about all the facts the girls had gathered, even now.

After that Neale seemed more afraid than ever of meeting somebody on the public streets. Agnes and Ruth knew that he never went out evenings, save to climb over the fence and come to the old Corner House.

He was spending more time at his books, having earned a nice little sum during the winter taking care of furnaces and shoveling paths. That work was past now, and he said he had enough money to keep him comfortably until the end of the school year.

It was another Saturday. Neale had driven out into the country for a neighbor, but had promised to come to the old Corner House about four o'clock. Almost always he took supper Saturday evening with the girls. Mrs. MacCall usually had fishcakes and baked beans, and Neale was extravagantly fond of that homely New England combination.

As it chanced, none of the four Kenways but Ruth went shopping that afternoon. It was warm enough for Tess and Dot to have their dolls out in the summer-house. They had set up house-keeping there for the season and were very busy.

Agnes had found a book that she enjoyed immensely, and she was wrapped up in an old coat and hidden in a crotch of the Baldwin appletree behind the woodshed. She was so deeply absorbed that she did not wake to the click of the gate-latch and did not realize there was a stranger in the yard until she heard a heavy boot on the brick walk.

"Hello, my gal!" said a rough voice. "Ain't none of the folks to home?"

Agnes dropped the book and sprang down from the appletree in a hurry. There at the corner of the shed stood a man in varnished top boots, with spurs in the heels—great, cruel looking spurs—velveteen breeches, a short, dirty white flannel coat, and a hard hat—something between a stovepipe and a derby. Agnes realized that it was some kind of a riding costume that he wore, and he lashed his bootleg with his riding whip as he talked.

He was such a red-faced man, and he was so stout and rough looking, that Agnes scarcely knew how to speak to him. She noted, too, that he had a big seal ring on one finger and that a heavy gold watchchain showed against his waistcoat where the short jacket was cut away.

"Who—who are you?" Agnes managed to stammer at last. "And what do you want?"

"Why, I'm Sorber, I am," said the man. "Sorber, of Twomley & Sorber's Herculean Circus and Menagerie. And my errand here is to git hold of a chap that's run away from me and my partner. I hear he's in Milton, and I come over from our winter quarters, out o' which we're going to git instanter, Miss; and they tells me down to that newspaper office that I kin find him here.

"Now, Miss, where is that 'circus boy' as they call him? Neale Sorber—that's his name. And I'm goin' to take him away with me."

CHAPTER XXIII

TAMING A LION TAMER

Agnes was both frightened and angry as she listened to the man in the topboots. He was such a coarse, rude fellow (or so she decided on the instant) that she found herself fairly hating him!

Beside, she was well aware that he referred to Neale O'Neil. He had come for Neale. He threatened to beat Neale with every snap of his heavy riding whip along the leg of his shiny boots. He was a beast!

That is what Agnes told herself. She was quick to jump at conclusions; but she was not quick to be disloyal to her friends.

Nor was she frightened long; especially not when she was angry. She would not tremble before this man, and she gained complete control of herself ere she spoke again. She was not going to deliver Neale O'Neil into his hands by any mistake of speech—no, indeed!

The name of Twomley & Sorter's Herculean Circus and Menagerie struck a cord of memory in Agnes' mind. It was one of the two shows that had exhibited at Milton the season before.

This man said that Neale had run away from this show. He claimed his name was really Neale Sorber!

And all the time Neale had denied any knowledge of circuses. Or, *had* he done just that? Agnes' swift thought asked the question and answered it. Neale had denied ever having attended a circus as a spectator. That might easily be true!

Agnes' voice was quite unshaken as she said to the red-faced man: "I don't think the person you are looking for is here, sir."

"Oh, yes he is! can't fool me," said the circus man, assuredly. "Young scamp! He run away from his lawful guardeens and protectors. I'll show him!" and he snapped the whiplash savagely again.

"He sha'n't show him in *that* way if I can help it," thought Agnes. But all she said aloud was: "There is no boy living here."

"Heh? how's that, Miss?" said Sorber, suspiciously.

Agnes repeated her statement.

"But you know where he does hang out?" said Sorber, slily, "I'll be bound!"

"I don't know that I do," Agnes retorted, desperately. "And if I did know, I wouldn't tell you!"

The man struck his riding boot sharply again. "What's that? what's that?" he growled.

Agnes' pluck was rising. "I'm not afraid of you—so there!" she said, bobbing her head at him.

"Why, bless you, Miss!" ejaculated Sorber. "I should hope not. I wouldn't hurt you for a farm Down East with a pig on it—no, Ma'am! We keep whips for the backs of runaways— not for pretty little ladies like you."

"You wouldn't *dare* beat Neale O'Neil!" gasped Agnes.

"Ah-ha?" exclaimed the man. "'Neale O'Neil?' Then you do know him?"

Agnes was stricken dumb with apprehension. Her anger had betrayed Neale, she feared.

"So that's what he calls himself, is it?" repeated Sorber. "O'Neil was his father's name. I didn't think he would remember."

"We can't be talking about the same boy," blurted out Agnes, trying to cover her "bad break." "You say his name is Sorber."

"Oh, he could take any name. I thought maybe he'd call himself 'Jakeway.' He was called 'Master Jakeway' on the bills and he'd oughter be proud of the name. We had too many Sorbers in the show. Sorber, ringmaster and lion tamer—that's *me*, Miss. Sully Sorber, first clown—that's my half brother, Miss. William Sorber is treasurer and ticket seller—under bonds, Miss. He's my own brother. And—until a few years ago—there was Neale's mother. She was my own sister."

Agnes had begun to be very curious. And while he was talking, the girl was looking Sorber over for a second time.

He was not all bad! Of that Agnes began to be sure. Yet he wanted to beat Neale O'Neil for running away from a circus.

To tell the truth, Agnes could scarcely understand how a boy could so dislike circus life as to really *want* to run away from even Twomley & Sorber's Herculean Circus and Menagerie. There was a glitter and tinsel to the circus that ever appealed to Agnes herself!

Personally Mr. Sorber lost none of his coarseness on longer acquaintance, but now Agnes noticed that there were humorous wrinkles about his eyes, and an upward twist to the corners of his mouth. She believed after all he might be good-natured.

Could she help Neale in any way by being friendly with this man? She could try. There was a rustic bench under the Baldwin tree.

"Won't you sit down, Mr. Sorber?" suggested Agnes, politely.

"Don't care if I do, Miss," declared the showman, and took an end of the bench, leaving the other end invitingly open, but Agnes leaned against the tree trunk and watched him.

"A nice old place you've got here. They tell me it's called 'the Old Corner House.' That's the way I was directed here. And so that rascal of mine's been here all winter? Nice, soft spot he fell into."

"It was I that came near falling," said Agnes, gravely, "and it wasn't a soft spot at all under that tree. I'd have been hurt if it hadn't been for Neale."

"Hel-*lo*!" exclaimed Neale's uncle, sharply. "What's this all about? That rascal been playin' the hero again? My, my! It ought to be a big drawin' card when we play this town in August. He always *was* a good number, as Master Jakeway in high and lofty tumbling; when he rode bareback; or doing the Joey—"

"The Joey?" repeated the girl, interested, but puzzled.

"That's being a clown, Miss. He has doubled as clown and bareback when we was short of performers and having a hard season."

"Our Neale?" gasped Agnes.

"Humph! Dunno about his being *yours*," said Sorber, with twinkling eyes. "He's mine, I reckon, by law."

Agnes bit her lip. It made her angry to have Sorber talk so confidently about his rights over poor Neale.

"Let me tell you how he came here," she said, after a moment, "and what he's done since he came to Milton."

"Fire away, Miss," urged the showman, clasping his pudgy hands, on a finger of one of them showing the enormous seal ring.

Agnes "began at the beginning," for once. She did not really know why she did so, but she gave the particulars of all that had happened to Neale—as she knew them—since he had rushed in at that gate the man had so lately entered and saved her from falling into the big peachtree by the bedroom window.

Mr. Sorber's comments as she went along, were characteristic. Sometimes he chuckled and nodded, anon he scowled, and more than once he rapped his bootleg soundly with the whip.

"The little rascal!" he said at last. "And he could have stayed with us, hived up as us'al in the winter with only the critters to nuss and tend, and been sure of his three squares.

"What does he rather do, but work and slave, and almost freeze and starve—jest to git what, I ax ye?"

"An education, I guess," said Agnes, mildly.

"Huh!" grunted Sorber. Then he was silent; but after a while he said: "His father all over again. Jim O'Ncil was a kid-gloved chap. If he could have let drink alone, he never would have come down to us show people.

"Huh! Well, my sister was as good as he was. And she stayed in the business all her life. And what was good enough for Jim O'Neil's wife was good enough for his kid—and is good enough to-day. Now I've got him, and I'm a-going to lug him back—by the scruff of the neck, if need be!"

Agnes felt her lip trembling. What should she do? If Neale came right away, this awful man would take him away—as he said—"by the scruff of his neck."

And what would happen to poor Neale? What would ever become of him? And Miss Georgiana was so proud of him. Mr. Marks had praised him. He was going to graduate into high school in June—

"And he shall!" thought the Corner House girl with an inspired determination. "Somehow I'll find a way to tame this lion tamer—see if I don't!"

"Well, Miss, you'd better perduce the villain," chuckled Mr. Sorber. "If he goes peaceable, we'll let bygones be bygones. He's my own sister's child. And Twomley says for me not to come back without him. I tell ye, he's a drawin' card, and no mistake."

"But, Mr. Sorber!" cried Agnes. "He wants to study so."

"Shucks! I won't stop him. He's allus readin' his book. I ain't never stopped him. Indeed, I've give him money many a time to buy a book when I needed the chink myself for terbacker."

"But—"

"And Twomley said I was doin' wrong. Less the boy learned, less he'd be like his father. And I expect Twomley's right."

"What was the matter with Neale's father?" questioned Agnes, almost afraid that she was overstepping the bounds of decency in asking. But curiosity—and interest in Neale— urged her on.

"He couldn't content himself in the show business. He was the high-tonedest ringmaster we ever had. I was only actin' the lions and a den of hyenas in them days. But I cut out the hyenas. You can't tame them brutes, and a man's got to have eyes in the back of his head and in his elbers, to watch 'em.

"Well! Jim O'Neil was a good-looker, and the Molls buzzed round him like bees round a honey pot. My sister was one of them and I'll say him fair—Jim O'Neil never raised his hand to her.

"But after the boy come he got restless. Said it was no life for a kid. Went off finally—to Klondike, or somewhere—to make his fortune. Never heard of him since. Of course he's dead or he'd found us, for lemme tell you, Miss, the repertation of Twomley & Sorber's Herculean Circus and Menagerie ain't a light hid under a bushel—by no manner o' means!"

Not if Mr. Sorber were allowed to advertise it, that was sure. But the man went on:

"So there you have it. Neale's mine. I'm his uncle. His mother told me when she was dying to look after him. And I'm a-going to. Now trot him out, Miss," and Mr. Sorber mopped his bald brow under the jaunty stiff hat. He was quite breathless.

"But I haven't him here, sir," said Agnes. "He doesn't live here."

"He ain't here?"

"No. He is living near. But he is not at home now."

"Now, see here—"

"I never tell stories," said Agnes, gravely.

Mr. Sorber had the grace to blush. "I dunno as I doubt ye, Miss—"

"We expect Neale here about four o'clock. Before that my sister Ruth will be at home. I want you to stay and see her, Mr. Sorber—"

"Sure I'll meet her," said Mr. Sorber, warmly. "I don't care if I meet every friend Neale's made in this man's town. But that don't make no differ. To the Twomley & Sorber tent show he belongs, and that's where he is a-goin' when I leave this here town to-night."

CHAPTER XXIV

MR. MURPHY TAKES A HAND

Agnes Kenway was pretty near at her wit's end. She did not know how to hold Mr. Sorber, and she did not dare to let him go away from the house, for he might meet Neale O'Neil on the road and take him right away from Milton.

If Agnes could help it, she was determined that their friend Neale should not be obliged to leave town just as he was getting on so well. She wanted to consult Ruth. Ruth, she believed, would know just how to handle this ticklish situation.

Just then Tess and Dot appeared, taking a walk through the yard with their very best dolls. Naturally they were surprised to see Agnes talking in the backyard with a strange man, and both stopped, curiously eyeing Mr. Sorber. Dot's finger involuntarily sought the corner of her mouth. *That* was a trick that she seemed never to grow out of.

"Hello!" said Mr. Sorber, with rough joviality, "who are these little dames? Goin' to say how-de-do to old Bill Sorber?"

Tess, the literal, came forward with her hand outstretched.

"How do you do, Mr. Sorber," she said.

Dot was a little bashful. But Agnes, having a brilliant idea, said:

"This is Neale's uncle, Dot. Mr. Sorber has come here to see him."

At that Dot came forward and put her morsel of hand into the showman's enormous fist.

"You are very welcome, Neale's uncle," she said, bashfully. "We think Neale is a very nice boy, and if we had a boy in our family we'd want one just like Neale—wouldn't we, Tess?"

"Ye-es," grudgingly admitted the older girl. "If we *had* to have a boy. But, you know, Dot, we haven't *got* to have one."

Mr. Sorber chuckled. "Don't you think boys are any good, little lady?" he asked Tess.

"Not so very much," said the frank Tess. "Of course, Neale is different, sir. He—he can harness Billy Bumps, and—and he can turn cartwheels—and—and he can climb trees—and—and do lots of things perfectly well. There aren't many boys like him."

"I guess there ain't," agreed Mr. Sorber. "And does he ever tell you how he was took into the Lions' Den, like a little Dan'l, when he was two, with spangled pants on him and a sugar lollypop to keep him quiet?"

"Mercy!" gasped Agnes.

"In a lions' den?" repeated Tess, while Dot's pretty eyes grew so round they looked like gooseberries.

"Yes, Ma'am! I done it. And it made a hit. But the perlice stopped it. Them perlice," said Mr. Sorber, confidentially, "are allus butting in where they ain't wanted."

"Like Billy Bumps," murmured Dot.

But Tess had struck a new line of thought and she wanted to follow it up. "Please, sir," she asked, "is that your business?"

"What's my business?"

"Going into lions' dens?"

"That's it. I'm a lion tamer, I am. And that's what I wanted to bring my nevvy up to, only his mother kicked over the traces and wouldn't have it."

"My!" murmured Tess. "It must be a very int'resting business. Do—do the lions ever bite?"

"They chews their food reg'lar," said Mr. Sorber gravely, but his eyes twinkled. "But none of 'em's ever tried to chew me. I reckon I look purty tough to 'em."

"And Neale's been in a den of lions and never told us about it?" gasped Agnes, in spite of herself carried away with the romantic side of the show business again.

"Didn't he ever?"

"He never told us he was with a circus at all," confessed Agnes. "He was afraid of being sent back, I suppose."

"And ain't he ever blowed about it to the boys?"

"Oh, no! He hasn't even told the school principal—or the man he lives with—or Ruth—or *anybody*," declared Agnes.

Mr. Sorber looked really amazed. He mopped his bald crown again and the color in his face deepened.

"Why, whizzle take me!" ejaculated the showman, in surprise, "he's ashamed of us!"

Tess's kindly little heart came to the rescue immediately. "Oh, he couldn't be ashamed of his uncle, sir," she said. "And Neale is, really, a very nice boy. He would not be ashamed of any of his relations. No, sir."

"Well, mebbe not," grumbled Mr. Sorber; "but it looks mightily like it."

Despite the roughness and uncouth manner of the man, the children "got under his skin" as the saying is. Soon Tess and Dot bore the old showman off to the summer-house to introduce him to their entire family.

At that moment Ruth arrived—to Agnes' vast relief.

"Oh, Ruthie!" the second Corner House girl gasped. "It's come!"

"What's come?" asked Ruth, in amazement.

"What Mr. Con Murphy said would happen some day. It's all out about Neale—Poor Neale! The dam's busted!"

It was several minutes before Ruth could get any clear account from her sister of what had happened. But when she *did* finally get into the story, Agnes told it lucidly—and she held Ruth's undivided attention, the reader may be sure.

"Poor Neale indeed!" murmured Ruth.

"What can we do?" demanded Agnes.

"I don't know. But surely, there must be some way out. I—I'll telephone to Mr. Howbridge."

"Oh, Ruthie! I never thought of that," squealed Agnes. "But suppose Neale comes before you can get Mr. Howbridge here?"

Ruth put on her thinking cap. "I tell you," she said. "Introduce me to Mr. Sorber. Get him to promise to stay to supper with Neale. That will give us time."

This plot was carried out. Ruth saw Mr. Sorber, too, under a much more favorable light. Dolls were much too tame for Dot and Tess, when they realized that they had a real live lion tamer in their clutches. So they had Mr. Sorber down on a seat in the corner of the summer-house, and he was explaining to them just how the lions looked, and acted—even how they roared.

"It's lots more int'resting than going to the circus to see them," Dot said, reflectively. "For *then* you're so scared of them that you can't remember how they look. But Mr. Sorber is a perfectly *safe* lion. He's even got false teeth. He told us so."

Mr. Sorber could scarcely refuse Ruth's invitation. He was much impressed by the appearance of the oldest Corner House girl.

"I reckon that rascally nevvy of mine has been playin' in great luck since he run away from Twomley & Sorber's Herculean Circus and Menagerie. Shouldn't blame him if he wanted to stay on. I'd wanter myself. Pleased to meet you, Miss."

Ruth hurried to the nearest telephone and called up the lawyer's office. She was not much surprised to find that he was not there, it being Saturday afternoon.

So then she called up the house where he lived. After some trouble she learned that her guardian had left town for over Sunday. She was told where he had gone; but Ruth did not feel it would be right to disturb him at a distance about Neale's affairs.

"Whom shall I turn to for help?" thought Ruth. "Who will advise us? Above all, who will stop this man Sorber from taking Neale away?"

She had a reckless idea of trying to meet Neale on the road and warn him. He could hide—until Mr. Howbridge got back, at least.

Perhaps she could catch Neale at the cobbler's house. And then, at thought of the queer little old Irishman, all Ruth's worry seemed to evaporate. Mr. Con Murphy was the man to attend to this matter. And to the cobbler's little cottage she immediately made her way.

The story she told the little Irishman made him drop the shoe he was at work upon and glare at her over his spectacles, and with his scant reddish hair ruffled up. This, with his whiskers, made him look like a wrathful cockatoo.

"Phat's that?" he cried, at last. "Take Neale O'Neil to a dirthy circus-show and make him do thricks, like a thrained pig, or a goose, or a—a—a naygur man from the Sahara Desert? NOT MUCH, SAYS CON!"

He leaped up and tore off his leather apron.

"The ormadhoun! I'd like a brush wid him, mesilf. Con Murphy takes a hand in this game. We nade no lawyer-body—not yit. Lave it to me, Miss Ruthie, acushla! Sure I'll invite mesilf to supper wid youse, too. I'll come wid Neale, and he shall be prepared beforehand. Be sure he comes here first. Never weep a tear, me dear. I'll fix thim circus people."

"Oh, Mr. Murphy! can you help us? Are you sure?" cried Ruth.

"Never fear! never fear!" returned the cobbler. "Lave it to me. Whin Con Murphy takes a hand in any game, he knows what he's about. And there's more than two sides to this mather, Miss Ruth. Belike thim fellers want Neale for the money he makes for them. Hear me, now! Before I'd lit thim take him back to that show, I'd spind ivry penny I've got buried in the ould sock in—Well, niver mind where," concluded the excited cobbler.

But where was Ruth to find Neale O'Neil? That was the question that faced the oldest Corner House girl as she turned away from the door of the little cobbler's shop. She feared right now that the boy might have returned to town and stopped at the Corner House to give the children a ride before returning to the stable the horses he drove.

For Neale O'Neil was very fond of Tess and Dot and never missed a chance of giving them pleasure. Although Ruth Kenway professed no high regard for boys of any descrip-tion—with Tess, she felt thankful there were none "in the family"—she had to admit that the boy who had run away from the circus was proving himself a good friend and companion.

Many of the good times the Corner House girls had enjoyed during the fall and winter just past, would have been impossible without Neale's assistance. He had been Agnes' and her own faithful cavalier at all times and seasons. His secret—that which had borne so heavily upon his heart—had sometimes made Ruth doubtful of him; but now that the truth was out, he had only the girl's sympathy and full regard.

"He sha'n't go back!" she told herself, as she hurried around the corner into Willow Street. "This horrid circus man shall not take him back. Oh! if Mr. Murphy can only do all that he says he can—"

Her heart had fallen greatly, once she was out from under the magnetism of the old cobbler's glistening eye. Mr. Sorber was such a big, determined, red-faced man! How could the little cobbler overcome such an opponent! He was another David against a monster Goliath.

And so Ruth's former idea returned to her. Neale must be stopped! He must be warned before he returned from the drive he had taken into the country, and before running right into the arms of his uncle.

This determination she arrived at before she reached the side gate of the Old Corner House premises. She called Agnes, and left the two younger children to play hostesses and amuse the guest.

"He mustn't suspect—he mustn't know," she whispered to Agnes, hurriedly. "You go one way, Aggie, and I'll go the other. Neale must return by either the Old Ridge Road or Ralph Avenue. Which one will you take?"

Agnes was just as excited as her older sister. "I'll go up Ral-Ralph Avenue, Ru-Ruth!" she gasped. "Oh! It will be dreadful if that awful Sorber takes away our Neale—"

"He sha'n't!" declared the older girl, starting off at once for the Old Ridge Road.

They had said nothing to Mrs. MacCall about the coming of Mr. Sorber—not even to tell the good housekeeper of the Old Corner House that she would have company at supper. But Mrs. MacCall found that out herself.

Finding Tess and Dot remarkably quiet in the garden, and for a much longer time than usual, Mrs. MacCall ventured forth to see what had happened to the little girls. She came to the summer-house in time to hear the following remarkable narrative:

"Why, ye see how it was, little ladies, ye see how it was. I saw the folks in that town didn't like us—not a little bit. Some country folks *don't* like circus people."

"I wonder why?" asked Tess, breathlessly.

"Don't know, don't know," said Mr. Sorber. "Just born with a nateral *hate* for us, I guess. Anyway, I seen there was likely to be a big clem—that's what we say for 'fight' in the show business—and I didn't get far from the lions—no, ma'am!"

"Were you afraid some of the bad men might hurt your lions, sir?" asked Dot, with anxiety.

"You can't never tell what a man that's mad is going to do," admitted the old showman, seriously. "I wasn't going to take any chances with 'em. About a wild animal you can tell. But mad folks are different!

"So I kept near the lion den; and when the row broke out and the roughs from the town began to fight our razorbacks—them's our pole - and canvas-men," explained Mr. Sorber, parenthetically, "I popped me right into the cage—yes, ma'am!

"Old Doublepaws and the Rajah was some nervous, and was traveling back and forth before the bars. They was disturbed by the racket. But they knowed me, and I felt a whole lot safer than I would have outside.

"'The show's a fake!' was what those roughs was crying. 'We want our money back!' But that was a wicked story," added Mr. Sorber, earnestly. "We was giving them a *big* show for their money. We had a sacred cow, a white elephant, and a Wild Man of Borneo that you couldn't have told from the real thing—he was dumb, poor fellow, and so the sounds he made when they prodded him sounded just as wild as wild could be!

"But you can't satisfy *some* folks," declared Mr. Sorber, warmly. "And there those roughs was shouting for their money. As I was telling you, I doubled, selling tickets and putting the lions through their paces. I'd taken the cashbox with me when I run for cover at the beginning of the trouble, and I'd brought it into the lions' cage with me.

"Twomley tried to pacify the gang, but it was no use. They were going to tear the big top down. That's the main tent, little ladies.

"So I knocks Old Doublepaws and Rajah aside—they was tame as kittens, but roared awful savage when I hit 'em—and I sings out:

"'Here's your money, ladies and gentlemen. Them that wants theirs back please enter the cage. One at a time, and no crowding, gents—' Haw! haw! haw!" exploded the show-man. "And how many do you suppose of them farmers come after their money? Not one, little ladies! not one!"

"So the lions saved your money for you?" quoth Tess, agreeably. "That's most int'resting—isn't it, Dot?"

"I—I wouldn't ever expect them to be so kind from the way they roar," announced the littlest Corner House girl, honestly. She had a vivid remembrance of the big cats that she had seen in the circus the previous summer.

"They're like folks—to a degree," said Mr. Sorber, soberly. "Some men is all gruff and bluff, but tender at heart. So's— Why, how-d'ye-do, ma'am!" he said, getting up and bowing to Mrs. MacCall, whom he just saw. "I hope I see you well?"

The housekeeper was rather amazed—as well she might have been; but Tess, who had a good, memory, introduced the old showman quite as a matter of course.

"This is Neale's uncle, Mrs. MacCall," she said. "Neale doesn't know he is here yet; but Ruthie has asked him to stay to supper—"

"With your permission, ma'am," said Mr. Sorber, with another flourish of his hat.

"Oh, to be sure," agreed the housekeeper.

"And Neale runned away from a circus when he came here," said the round-eyed Dot.

"No!" gasped the housekeeper.

"Yes, Mrs. MacCall," Tess hurried on to say. "And he used

to be a clown, and an acrobat, and—"

"And a lion in a Daniel's den!" interposed Dot, afraid that Tess would tell it all. "Did you *ever*?"

And Mrs. MacCall was sure she never had!

Meanwhile Ruth and Agnes had run their separate ways. It was Agnes who was fortunate in meeting the carriage driven by Neale O'Neil. The boy was alone, and the moment he saw the panting girl he drew in his horses. He knew something of moment had happened.

"What's brought you 'way out here, Aggie?" he demanded, turning the wheel so that she might climb in beside him. His passengers had been left in the country and he was to drive back for them late in the evening.

"It—it's *you*, Neale!" burst out Agnes, almost crying.

"What's the matter with me?" demanded the boy, in wonder.

"What you've been expecting has happened. Oh dear, Neale! whatever shall we do? Your Uncle Sorber's come for you."

The boy pulled in his team with a frightened jerk, and for a moment Agnes thought he was going to jump from the carriage. She laid a hand upon his arm.

"But we're not going to let him take you away, Neale! Oh, we won't! Ruth says we must hide you—somewhere. She's gone out the Old Ridge Road to meet you."

"She'll get lost out that way," said the boy, suddenly. "She's never been over that way, has she?"

"Never mind—Ruth," Agnes said. "It's you we're thinking of—"

"We'll drive around and get Ruth," Neale said, decisively, and he began to turn the horses.

"Oh, Neale!" groaned Agnes. "What an *awful* man your uncle must be. He says he used to put you in a cage full of lions—"

Neale O'Neil suddenly began to laugh. Agnes looked at him in surprise. For a moment—as she told Ruth afterward—she was afraid that the shock of what she had told him about Mr. Sorber's appearance, had "sort of turned his brain."

"Why, Neale!" she exclaimed.

"Those poor, old, toothless, mangy beasts," chuckled Neale. "They had to be poked up half an hour before the crowd came in, or they wouldn't act their part at all. And half the time when the crowd thought the lions were opening their mouths savagely, they were merely yawning."

"Don't!" gasped Agnes. "You'll spoil every menagerie I ever see if you keep talking that way."

The laugh seemed to bring Neale back to a better mind. He sighed and then shrugged his shoulders. "We'll find Ruth," he said, with determination, "and then drive home. I'll see what Mr. Murphy says, and then see Mr. Sorber."

"But he's come to take you away, Neale!" cried Agnes.

"What good will it do for me to run? He knows I'm here,"

said the boy, hopelessly. "It would spoil my chance at school if I hid out somewhere. No; I've got to face him. I might as well do so now."

CHAPTER XXV

A BRIGHT FUTURE

That Saturday night supper at the old Corner House was rather different from any that had preceded it. Frequently the Corner House girls had company at this particular meal— almost always Neale, and Mr. Con Murphy had been in before.

Once Miss Shipman, Agnes' and Neale's teacher, had come as the guest of honor; and more than once Mr. Howbridge had passed his dish for a second helping of Mrs. MacCall's famous beans.

It was an elastic table, anyway, that table of the Corner House girls. It was of a real cozy size when the family was alone. Mrs. MacCall sat nearest the swing-door into the butler's pantry, although Uncle Rufus would seldom hear to the housekeeper going into the kitchen after she had once seated herself at the table.

She always put on a clean apron and cap. At the other end of the table was Aunt Sarah's place. No matter how grim and speechless Aunt Sarah might be, she could not glare Mrs. MacCall out of countenance, so that arrangement was very satisfactory.

The four girls had their seats, two on either side. The guests, when they had them, were placed between the girls on either side, and the table was gradually drawn out, and leaves added, to suit the circumstances.

Neale always sat between Tess and Dot. He did so to-night. But beside him was the Irish cobbler. Opposite was the stout and glowing Mr. Sorber, prepared to do destruction to Mrs. MacCall's viands first of all, and then to destroy Neale's hopes of an education afterward.

At least, he had thus far admitted no change of heart. He had met Neale with rough cordiality, but he had stated his intention as irrevocable that he would take the boy back to the circus.

Tess and Dot were almost horrified when they came to understand that their friend the lion tamer proposed to take Neale away. They could not understand such an evidently kind-hearted tamer of wild beasts doing such a cruel thing!

"I guess he's only fooling," Tess confided to Dot, and the latter agreed with several nods, her mouth being too full for utterance, if her heart was not.

"These beans," declared Mr. Sorber, passing his plate a third time, "are fit for a king to eat, and the fishcakes ought to make any fish proud to be used up in that manner. I never eat better, Ma'am!"

"I presume you traveling people have to take many meals haphazardly," suggested Mrs. MacCall.

"Not much. My provender," said Mr. Sorber, "is one thing that I'm mighty particular about. I feeds my lions first; then Bill Sorber's next best friend is his own stomach—

yes, Ma'am!

"The cook tent and the cooks go ahead of the show. For instance, right after supper the tent is struck and packed, and if we're traveling by rail, it goes right aboard the first flat. If we go by road, that team gets off right away and when we catch up to it in the morning, it's usually set up on the next camping ground and the coffee is a-biling.

"It ain't no easy life we live; but it ain't no dog's life, neither. And how a smart, bright boy like this here nevvy of mine should want to run away from it—"

"Did ye iver think, sir," interposed the cobbler, softly, "that mebbe there was implanted in the la-ad desires for things ye know nothin' of?"

"Huh!" grunted Sorber, balancing a mouthful of beans on his knife to the amazement of Dot, who had seldom seen any person eat with his knife.

"Lit me speak plainly, for 'tis a plain man I am," said the Irishman. "This boy whom ye call nephew—?"

"And he is," Sorber said.

"Aye. But he has another side to him that has no Sorber to it. 'Tis the O'Neil side. It's what has set him at his books till he is the foinest scholar in the Milton Schools, bar none. Mr. Marks told me himself 'twas so."

This surprised Neale and the girls for they had not known how deep was the Irishman's interest in his protege.

"He's only half a Sorber, sir. Ye grant that?"

"But he's been with the show since he was born," growled the showman. "Why shouldn't he want to be a showman, too? All the Sorbers have been, since away back. I was thinkin' of changing his name by law so as to have him in the family in earnest."

"I'll never own to any name but my own again," declared Neale, from across the table.

"That's your answer, Mr. Sorber," declared Murphy, earnestly. "The boy wants to go his own way—and that's the way of his fathers, belike. But I'm a fair man. I can see 'tis a loss to you if Neale stays here and goes to school."

"I guess it is, Mister," said the showman, rather belligerently. "And I guess you don't know how much of a loss."

"Well," said the cobbler, coolly. "Put a figure to it. How much?"

"How much *what*?" demanded Mr. Sorber, bending his brows upon the Irishman, while the children waited breathlessly.

"Money. Neale's a big drawin' kyard ye say yerself. Then, how much money will ye take for your right to him?"

Mr. Sorber laid down his knife and fork and stared at Mr. Murphy.

"Do you mean that, sir?" he asked, with strange quietness.

"Do I mean am I willin' to pay the bye out of yer clutches?" demanded the cobbler, with growing heat. "'Deed and I am! and if my pile isn't big enough, mebbe I kin find good friends of Neale O'Neil in this town that'll be glad to chip in wid me and give the bye his chance.

"I've been layin' a bit av money by, from year to year—God knows why! for I haven't chick nor child in the wor-r-rld. Save the bit to kape me from the potter's field and to pay for sayin' a mass for me sowl, what do the likes of *me* want wid hoardin' gold and silver?

"I'll buy a boy. I have no son of me own. I'll see if Neale shall not do me proud in the years to come—God bliss the bye!"

He seized the boy's hand and wrung it hard. "Oh, Mr. Murphy!" murmured Neale O'Neil and returned the pressure of the cobbler's work-hardened palm.

But Agnes got up and ran around the table and hugged him! "You—you are the dearest old man who ever lived, Mr. Murphy!" she sobbed, and implanted a tearful kiss right upon the top of the cobbler's little snub nose!

"Huh!" grunted Mr. Sorber. Then he said "Huh!" again. Finally he burst out with: "Say, young lady, ain't you going to pass around some of those kisses? Don't *I* get one?"

"What?" cried Agnes, turning in a fury. "*Me* kiss *you*?"

"Sure. Why not?" asked the showman. "You don't suppose that man sitting there is the only generous man in the world, do you? Why, bless your heart! I want Neale back bad enough. And he *does* make us a tidy bit of money each season—and some of *that's* to his credit in the bank—I've seen to it myself.

"He's my own sister's boy. I—I used to play with him when he was a little bit of a feller—don't you remember them times, Neale?"

"Yes, sir," said the boy, with hanging head. "But I'm too big for play now. I want to learn—I want to know."

Mr. Sorber looked at him a long time. He had stopped eating, and had dropped the napkin which he had tucked under his chin. Finally he blew a big sigh.

"Well, Mr. Murphy," he said. "Put up your money. You've not enough to *buy* the boy, no matter how much you have laid away. But if he feels that way—

"Well, what the Old Scratch I'll say to Twomley I don't know. But I'll leave the boy in your care. I'm stickin' by my rights, though. If he's a big success in this world, part of it'll be due to the way I trained him when he was little. There's no doubt of that."

* * * * *

So, that is the way it came about that Neale O'Neil remained at school in Milton and lost the "black dog of trouble" that had for months haunted his footsteps.

The Corner House girls were delighted at the outcome of the affair.

"If we grow to be as old as Mrs. Methuselah," declared Agnes, "we'll never be so happy as we are over this thing."

But, of course, that is an overstatement of the case. It was only a few weeks ahead that Agnes would declare herself surfeited with happiness again—and my readers may learn the reason why if they read the next volume of this series, entitled "The Corner House Girls Under Canvas."

Grace Brooks Hill

But this settlement of Neale's present affairs was really a very great occasion. Mr. Sorber and Mr. Con Murphy shook hands on the agreement. Mrs. MacCall wiped her eyes, declaring that "such goings-on wrung the tears out o' her jest like water out of a dishclout!"

What Aunt Sarah said was to the point, and typical: "For the marcy's sake! I never did see thet boys was either useful enough, or ornamental enough, to make such a fuss over 'em!"

Uncle Rufus, hovering on the outskirts of the family party, grinned hugely upon Neale O'Neil. "Yo' is sho' 'nuff too good a w'ite boy tuh be made tuh dance an' frolic in no circus show—naw-zer! I's moughty glad yo's got yo' freedom."

Neale, too, was glad. The four Corner House girls got around him, joined hands, and danced a dance of rejoicing in the big front hall.

"And now you need not be afraid of what's going to happen to you all the time," said Ruth, warmly.

"Oh, Neale! you'll tell us all about what happened to you in the circus, won't you, now?" begged Agnes.

"Will you please show me how to do cartwheels, Neale?" asked Tess, gravely. "I've always admired seeing boys do them."

But Dot capped the climax—as usual. "Neale," she said, with serious mien a day or two after, "if that circus comes to town this summer, will you show us how you played Little Daniel in the Lions' Den? I should think *that* would be real int'resting—and awfully religious!"

Choose from Thousands of 1stWorldLibrary Classics By

A. M. Barnard
Ada Leverson
Adolphus William Ward
Aesop
Agatha Christie
Alexander Aaronsohn
Alexander Kielland
Alexandre Dumas
Alfred Gatty
Alfred Ollivant
Alice Duer Miller
Alice Turner Curtis
Alice Dunbar
Allen Chapman
Alleyne Ireland
Ambrose Bierce
Amelia E. Barr
Amory H. Bradford
Andrew Lang
Andrew McFarland Davis
Andy Adams
Angela Brazil
Anna Alice Chapin
Anna Sewell
Annie Besant
Annie Hamilton Donnell
Annie Payson Call
Annie Roe Carr
Annonaymous
Anton Chekhov
Archibald Lee Fletcher
Arnold Bennett
Arthur C. Benson
Arthur Conan Doyle
Arthur M. Winfield
Arthur Ransome
Arthur Schnitzler
Arthur Train
Atticus
B.H. Baden-Powell
B. M. Bower
B. C. Chatterjee
Baroness Emmuska Orczy
Baroness Orczy
Basil King
Bayard Taylor
Ben Macomber
Bertha Muzzy Bower
Bjornstjerne Bjornson

Booth Tarkington
Boyd Cable
Bram Stoker
C. Collodi
C. E. Orr
C. M. Ingleby
Carolyn Wells
Catherine Parr Traill
Charles A. Eastman
Charles Amory Beach
Charles Dickens
Charles Dudley Warner
Charles Farrar Browne
Charles Ives
Charles Kingsley
Charles Klein
Charles Hanson Towne
Charles Lathrop Pack
Charles Romyn Dake
Charles Whibley
Charles Willing Beale
Charlotte M. Braeme
Charlotte M. Yonge
Charlotte Perkins Stetson
Clair W. Hayes
Clarence Day Jr.
Clarence E. Mulford
Clemence Housman
Confucius
Coningsby Dawson
Cornelis DeWitt Wilcox
Cyril Burleigh
D. H. Lawrence
Daniel Defoe
David Garnett
Dinah Craik
Don Carlos Janes
Donald Keyhoe
Dorothy Kilner
Dougan Clark
Douglas Fairbanks
E. Nesbit
E. P. Roe
E. Phillips Oppenheim
E. S. Brooks
Earl Barnes
Edgar Rice Burroughs
Edith Van Dyne
Edith Wharton

Edward Everett Hale
Edward J. O'Biren
Edward S. Ellis
Edwin L. Arnold
Eleanor Atkins
Eleanor Hallowell Abbott
Eliot Gregory
Elizabeth Gaskell
Elizabeth McCracken
Elizabeth Von Arnim
Ellem Key
Emerson Hough
Emilie F. Carlen
Emily Bronte
Emily Dickinson
Enid Bagnold
Enilor Macartney Lane
Erasmus W. Jones
Ernie Howard Pie
Ethel May Dell
Ethel Turner
Ethel Watts Mumford
Eugene Sue
Eugenie Foa
Eugene Wood
Eustace Hale Ball
Evelyn Everett-green
Everard Cotes
F. H. Cheley
F. J. Cross
F. Marion Crawford
Fannie E. Newberry
Federick Austin Ogg
Ferdinand Ossendowski
Fergus Hume
Florence A. Kilpatrick
Fremont B. Deering
Francis Bacon
Francis Darwin
Frances Hodgson Burnett
Frances Parkinson Keyes
Frank Gee Patchin
Frank Harris
Frank Jewett Mather
Frank L. Packard
Frank V. Webster
Frederic Stewart Isham
Frederick Trevor Hill
Frederick Winslow Taylor

Friedrich Kerst
Friedrich Nietzsche
Fyodor Dostoyevsky
G.A. Henty
G.K. Chesterton
Gabrielle E. Jackson
Garrett P. Serviss
Gaston Leroux
George A. Warren
George Ade
Geroge Bernard Shaw
George Cary Eggleston
George Durston
George Ebers
George Eliot
George Gissing
George MacDonald
George Meredith
George Orwell
George Sylvester Viereck
George Tucker
George W. Cable
George Wharton James
Gertrude Atherton
Gordon Casserly
Grace E. King
Grace Gallatin
Grace Greenwood
Grant Allen
Guillermo A. Sherwell
Gulielma Zollinger
Gustav Flaubert
H. A. Cody
H. B. Irving
H.C. Bailey
H. G. Wells
H. H. Munro
H. Irving Hancock
H. R. Naylor
H. Rider Haggard
H. W. C. Davis
Haldeman Julius
Hall Caine
Hamilton Wright Mabie
Hans Christian Andersen
Harold Avery
Harold McGrath
Harriet Beecher Stowe
Harry Castlemon
Harry Coghill
Harry Houidini

Hayden Carruth
Helent Hunt Jackson
Helen Nicolay
Hendrik Conscience
Hendy David Thoreau
Henri Barbusse
Henrik Ibsen
Henry Adams
Henry Ford
Henry Frost
Henry James
Henry Jones Ford
Henry Seton Merriman
Henry W Longfellow
Herbert A. Giles
Herbert Carter
Herbert N. Casson
Herman Hesse
Hildegard G. Frey
Homer
Honore De Balzac
Horace B. Day
Horace Walpole
Horatio Alger Jr.
Howard Pyle
Howard R. Garis
Hugh Lofting
Hugh Walpole
Humphry Ward
Ian Maclaren
Inez Haynes Gillmore
Irving Bacheller
Isabel Cecilia Williams
Isabel Hornibrook
Israel Abrahams
Ivan Turgenev
J.G.Austin
J. Henri Fabre
J. M. Barrie
J. M. Walsh
J. Macdonald Oxley
J. R. Miller
J. S. Fletcher
J. S. Knowles
J. Storer Clouston
J. W. Duffield
Jack London
Jacob Abbott
James Allen
James Andrews
James Baldwin

James Branch Cabell
James DeMille
James Joyce
James Lane Allen
James Lane Allen
James Oliver Curwood
James Oppenheim
James Otis
James R. Driscoll
Jane Abbott
Jane Austen
Jane L. Stewart
Janet Aldridge
Jens Peter Jacobsen
Jerome K. Jerome
Jessie Graham Flower
John Buchan
John Burroughs
John Cournos
John F. Kennedy
John Gay
John Glasworthy
John Habberton
John Joy Bell
John Kendrick Bangs
John Milton
John Philip Sousa
John Taintor Foote
Jonas Lauritz Idemil Lie
Jonathan Swift
Joseph A. Altsheler
Joseph Carey
Joseph Conrad
Joseph E. Badger Jr
Joseph Hergesheimer
Joseph Jacobs
Jules Vernes
Julian Hawthrone
Julie A Lippmann
Justin Huntly McCarthy
Kakuzo Okakura
Karle Wilson Baker
Kate Chopin
Kenneth Grahame
Kenneth McGaffey
Kate Langley Bosher
Kate Langley Bosher
Katherine Cecil Thurston
Katherine Stokes
L. A. Abbot
L. T. Meade

L. Frank Baum
Latta Griswold
Laura Dent Crane
Laura Lee Hope
Laurence Housman
Lawrence Beasley
Leo Tolstoy
Leonid Andreyev
Lewis Carroll
Lewis Sperry Chafer
Lilian Bell
Lloyd Osbourne
Louis Hughes
Louis Joseph Vance
Louis Tracy
Louisa May Alcott
Lucy Fitch Perkins
Lucy Maud Montgomery
Luther Benson
Lydia Miller Middleton
Lyndon Orr
M. Corvus
M. H. Adams
Margaret E. Sangster
Margret Howth
Margaret Vandercook
Margaret W. Hungerford
Margret Penrose
Maria Edgeworth
Maria Thompson Daviess
Mariano Azuela
Marion Polk Angellotti
Mark Overton
Mark Twain
Mary Austin
Mary Catherine Crowley
Mary Cole
Mary Hastings Bradley
Mary Roberts Rinehart
Mary Rowlandson
M. Wollstonecraft Shelley
Maud Lindsay
Max Beerbohm
Myra Kelly
Nathaniel Hawthrone
Nicolo Machiavelli
O. F. Walton
Oscar Wilde

Owen Johnson
P.G. Wodehouse
Paul and Mabel Thorne
Paul G. Tomlinson
Paul Severing
Percy Brebner
Percy Keese Fitzhugh
Peter B. Kyne
Plato
Quincy Allen
R. Derby Holmes
R. L. Stevenson
R. S. Ball
Rabindranath Tagore
Rahul Alvares
Ralph Bonehill
Ralph Henry Barbour
Ralph Victor
Ralph Waldo Emmerson
Rene Descartes
Ray Cummings
Rex Beach
Rex E. Beach
Richard Harding Davis
Richard Jefferies
Richard Le Gallienne
Robert Barr
Robert Frost
Robert Gordon Anderson
Robert L. Drake
Robert Lansing
Robert Lynd
Robert Michael Ballantyne
Robert W. Chambers
Rosa Nouchette Carey
Rudyard Kipling
Saint Augustine
Samuel B. Allison
Samuel Hopkins Adams
Sarah Bernhardt
Sarah C. Hallowell
Selma Lagerlof
Sherwood Anderson
Sigmund Freud
Standish O'Grady
Stanley Weyman
Stella Benson
Stella M. Francis

Stephen Crane
Stewart Edward White
Stijn Streuvels
Swami Abhedananda
Swami Parmananda
T. S. Ackland
T. S. Arthur
The Princess Der Ling
Thomas A. Janvier
Thomas A Kempis
Thomas Anderton
Thomas Bailey Aldrich
Thomas Bulfinch
Thomas De Quincey
Thomas Dixon
Thomas H. Huxley
Thomas Hardy
Thomas More
Thornton W. Burgess
U. S. Grant
Upton Sinclair
Valentine Williams
Various Authors
Vaughan Kester
Victor Appleton
Victor G. Durham
Victoria Cross
Virginia Woolf
Wadsworth Camp
Walter Camp
Walter Scott
Washington Irving
Wilbur Lawton
Wilkie Collins
Willa Cather
Willard F. Baker
William Dean Howells
William le Queux
W. Makepeace Thackeray
William W. Walter
William Shakespeare
Winston Churchill
Yei Theodora Ozaki
Yogi Ramacharaka
Young E. Allison
Zane Grey